Growing In Grace

Copyright © 2002 by Acts 20/20 Ministries

ISBN 978-0-578-01952-9

All rights reserved. No part of this publication may be reproduced, distributed, or transmitted in any form or by any means, including photocopying, recording, or other electronic or mechanical methods, without the prior written permission of the publisher, except in the case of brief quotations embodied in critical reviews and certain other noncommercial uses permitted by copyright law. For permission requests, write to the publisher:

Acts 20/20 Ministries
P.O. Box 75581
Colorado Springs, CO 80970

I asked Jesus to be my Lord on,

Date _____

Name _____

Address _____

_____

Phone number _____

My Lord has instructed me in II Timothy 2:15
To study to show myself approved unto God,
A workman that needeth not to be ashamed
Rightly dividing the Word of truth.
(KJV)

Foreword

We would like to welcome you to the Growing In Grace Bible Study, which is a basic introduction to the Kingdom of God.

We believe the Lord has instrumented this study so that you may grow in Him as smoothly and quickly as possible. There is nothing as important as a personal relationship with our Heavenly Father and our Lord and Savior, Jesus Christ.

The Lord has used many people to bring this manual to its present state and it has been made as user friendly as possible. By popular request it has been reduced in size so that it will be more convenient for travel, etc.

In this study we will examine God's New Covenant, what it means to be born again, how we fit into His Kingdom, and His fringe benefit package.

We will learn how much God loves us and through progressive growth we will learn how to deepen our relationship with Him and Jesus Christ.

We will also learn why a relationship with God, the creator of all things, is so much different from all other religions being practiced.

May all of us, grow in grace together.

Your Acts 20/20 Team

LESSON INDEX

LESSON 1

Examining, Being Born-Again
And The New Covenant 1-6
Hebrews 7:15-28 & 8:1-2 7
The Night Of The Last Supper 8-12
The Four Stages Of Spiritual Growth 13
In Him 14
You Can Receive Eternal Life Right Now 116-117

LESSON 2

Learning How To Study God's Word 15-17
So How Do We Study the Bible? 18-19
How To Sift God's Word From The Head To The Heart ... 20
Happy 21
God's Word Applied 22

LESSON 3

Learning How To Pray 23-27
II Peter 1:2-11 28
Applications Of Prayer 29
How To Approach God In Prayer 30
Taking A Stance of Faith, After We Have Prayed
The Prayer Of Faith 31-32

LESSON 4

The Devotional Life 33-36
What Is God's Snuggle Package? 37

LESSON 5

The Promise Of The Father: Versus The Gifts Of The Spirit 39-42
The Promise Of The Father: The Baptism With The Holy Spirit 43-46
The Promise Of The Father: Observations 47
The Holy Spirit: A Closer Look 48

GROWING IN GRACE
LESSON INDEX

LESSON 6

The Leadership Of The Holy Spirit 49-50
Let's Fine Tune – Training Our Spirit To Be Able To Listen
                To The Holy Spirit 51

LESSON 7

The Gifts Of The Holy Spirit 53-59

LESSON 8

Scriptural Healing 61-64
I Am 65

LESSON 9

The Fruit Of The Spirit 67-68
Galatians 5:13-26 69-70

LESSON 10

The Pathway to Inner Peace 71-72

LESSON 11

Work Out Your Own Salvation? 73-75
Happy 76

LESSON 12

Christian Warfare 77-80
The New Covenant Authority 81
The Prayer Of Binding And Loosing 82-83
Binding And Loosing In Daily Relationships 84

GROWING IN GRACE
LESSON INDEX

LESSON 13

Learning to Share God's Love	85-88
Five phases of Soul Winning	89
Evangelism Thoughts	90
The Top Ten Excuses	91-92
The Six Step Approach	93-94
Receive Eternal Life Now	116-117

LESSON 14

Water Baptism 95-98

LESSON 15

Holy Communion 99-102

LESSON 16

So, What About Tithing? 103-106

FAITH HELPS

Memory Work 107

"Come Unto Me"
Words To Remember 108

Faith Builders #1 109

Faith Builders #2 110

Stress Or Peace Of Mind 111

Your Heavenly Father Wants You To Remember 112

The Book of Jude 113-114

The Ten Commandments 115

GROWING IN GRACE
PRAYER STUDY INDEX

LESSON 1

Introduction And Building A Foundation To Prayer 23-32
The Night Of The Last Supper..8-12
Four Stages Of Spiritual Growth..13

LESSON 2

Applications Of Prayer..29
Scriptural Healing..61-64

LESSON 3

How To Approach God In Prayer..30
The Pathway to Inner Peace..71-72

LESSON 4

Taking A Stance Of Faith, While We Are Waiting On God's
                Answer To Our Prayer......................................31-32

LESSON 5

The Devotional Life..33-36
The Promise Of The Father...39-42
I Am 65

LESSON 6

Christian Warfare 77-80
The New Covenant Authority 81
Prayer Of Binding And Loosing 82-83
Binding And Loosing In Daily Relationships 84

There are additional helps in the Faith Help section in the back of this manual.

Lesson – 1

EXAMINING BEING BORN-AGAIN AND THE NEW COVENANT

THE FRINGE BENEFIT PACKAGE
FOR GOD'S CHIKDREN

1. We have been forgiven and cleansed from sin because, Jesus loved us enough, to go to the cross.

2. We have been given Eternal Life and have become JOINT HEIRS with Jesus God's Son.

3. We have been given the PROMISE of the Father which is, THE PERSON of the Holy Spirit. He is the one that recreates our inner spirit and then indwells us and fills us to over flowing when we let Him. (THE BAPTISM) He has been sent to guide, lead and teach us. Paul says, "that the person of the Holy Spirit is a surety (down payment) PAYMENT of all God has for us".

4. We have been given THE GIFTS of the Holy Spirit.

5. We have been given THE FRUIT of the Spirit which is, THE VERY CHARACTER and NATURE of GOD HIMSELF.

6. And you add to this, Galatians Chapter 5:13-14, where Paul says, "The PROMISES of Abraham BELONG to the gentiles as well".

7. The most IMPORTANT BENEFIT of all is, THE PROGRESSIVE, (GROWING IN GRACE) TWO WAY RELATIONSHIP, WITH YOUR HEAVENLY FATHER AND YOUR LORD AND SAVIOR JESUS CHRIST.

THE GROWING IN GRACE BIBLE STUDY

Welcome to the Growing in Grace Bible Study.

The goal of this study is to help you to be aware, that your Heavenly Father is trying to get your attention, and to challenge you in your spiritual growth, and to give you the Biblical tools needed to clear the debris of life, that has been blocking your direct pathway to your Heavenly Father.

- Your Heavenly Father is trying to show you, that you have direct access, to Him-self and to His Son, Jesus.

- You have been invited by the Father, the Creator of the universe, to be involved in His life, and He wants to be involved in your life.

- Jesus said in John chapter 4, "God is looking for people to WORSHIP HIM IN SPIRIT AND IN TRUTH".
  John 4:21-24

- The Lord said in Hebrews 4:16, "Come boldly to the Throne of Grace".

- The Lord wants you to study His Word. This is an important part of the process of getting to know Him. The Bible says in II Timothy 2:15, "Study to show yourself approved - -". God told Joshua, "to meditate on the Word day and night in order to be a good success", God wants you, to be a good success. Joshua 1:8

We are going to share a step-by-step pathway, to help you learn, to let the Holy Spirit guide, lead and teach you in your personal growth and relationship with the Father and Son. Look at John 16:7-15.

The Bible teaches that there are four stages to (in) our spiritual growth. Our spiritual growth is progressive, beginning as a babe in Christ, to becoming mature in Christ.

Turn to Ephesians chapter 1. Beginning with verses 16-23 and into chapter 3, verses 14-21, Paul is saying that our growth is through the inner man. In other words, the inner man has to grow to the point that it can control the outer man. The Bible separates the inner man and the outer man. The spiritual man in contrast to the natural (Carnal) man.

So this would answer your question, what do we do now, since we have become, Born-Again? The answer is, Prayer, Study and Application. James 1:22

There are 16 lessons, each one dealing with a specific area of spiritual growth. Each lesson will be an introduction to one of God's priorities in developing a personal relationship with Him. In all, this study represents, the *MINIMUM*, that our Heavenly Father desires for each of us to learn and for it to become a way of life.

The Tip of the ICE-BERG of God's provision for you.

May we take a few moments to review the Lesson Index at the front of this Manual. Please Turn to the Lesson Index and Preview the lessons and then return to this page.

We will begin with lesson ONE by discussing ----

- a. What does it mean to be Born-Again?
- b. How do we become Born-Again?
- c. What are the Benefits of being Born-Again?
- d. Why should we be Born-Again?
- e. What is the New Covenant?
- f. How did the New Covenant come into being?
- g. Why do we need a New Covenant with God?

Why are these two subjects so important?

- To establish, who we are and how we fit into the family of God. Look at the, In Him verses on page 14.

- To eliminate being tossed around by every wind of doctrine. James 1:1-8

To learn what our Heavenly Father expects of us. David said; I hide your Word in my heart, so that I will not sin against You.

- So that we may grow into the UNITY of Faith.

- To reduce or eliminate areas, where satan can attack us. God says; My people are destroyed because of their lack of knowledge.

What does it mean to be Born-Again?

We must look back to the time of creation in Genesis chapter 1:26-31. God created man in His spiritual image. God gave man's spirit a soul. Since God does not have a physical body as we know it, He formed our bodies out of the dust of the earth to house the spirit and soul. So, we are a spirit, soul and body.
(Genesis 1:26 & 2:7 and I Thessalonians 5:23)

The reason God created man is, that He desired (longed for) a people that would love Him for who He is and that He could have a two-way personal fellowship with them. At creation, man did have fellowship with God, but man lost that fellowship with God, when Adam and Eve sinned in the Garden of Eden.

How do we become Born-Again?

Jesus came to pay the price as, *the once and for all sacrifice on the cross* (Hebrews chapters 7-9). He came to show us that fellowship with God, could be reinstated through hearing the Gospel and responding to God's instructions. (Romans 10:9-10)

His instructions are: (The Basic Gospel) We must first recognize that we are sinners, then repent of our sins, and ask God to forgive us of our sins, and ask Jesus to come into our hearts to be our personal Savior. (I John.1:9) We should follow through and be baptized in water as quickly as we can, in obedience to the Lord's instructions in Acts 2:38-41.

Jesus said to Nicodemus, " You must be Born-Again".

Nicodemus responded, "How can that be?" This was a mystery to a prominent Religious Leader. John 3:1-21

When we respond to God's Word and ask God to forgive us our sin, and ask Jesus to come into our heart to be our Savior, the Holy Spirit that caused the virgin birth, and raised Jesus from the grave, enters our body and recreates our inner spirit.

Being "Born-Again" means, that God has recreated your inner spirit through the *POWER* of the Holy Spirit. He has come to live in you and to begin fellowship with you. He has now become, your Heavenly Father.

What are the benefits of being Born-Again?

1. We have been *FORGIVEN* and *CLEANSED* from sin.

2. We have been given *ETERNAL LIFE*.

3. We have been made *JOINT HEIRS* with God's Son, Jesus. Romans 8:17

4. We have been given the *PROMISE* of the Father, which is the *BAPTISM* in the Holy Spirit. This is, a PRIORITY of God, for us to seek.

5. We have been given the *GIFTS* of the Holy Spirit, in order to have a Balanced Body Ministry. I Corinthians chapter 12.

6. We have been given the *FRUIT* of the Spirit, which is the very *CHARACTER* and *NATURE* of God Himself. Galatians 5:16-25 and II Peter 1:3-4. (LVB)

7. We have been given the *SAME PROMISES* God gave to Abraham. Galatians 3:13-14

8. And most importantly, we have been given *DIRECT ACCESS* to God the Father and our Lord and Savior, Jesus Christ. John 16:7-15

Why should we be Born-Again?

- The Bible says that you must be Born-Again to enter into the Kingdom of Heaven *(John 3:3)*.

- Another reason is that all of the provisions listed previously do not become effective until you are Born-Again.

- By being *BORN-AGAIN*, we have now left religion and entered into a New Covenant relationship with God.

What is the New Covenant?

- The God Head, planned for the creation of man, before the creation of the earth.

- Jesus knew before the creation of the earth, that He would have to die on the cross.

- A history study of the Old Testament describes God's efforts to get man's attention and the many covenants that were made with man. Man always broke his side of the covenant.

- The last covenant between God and man in the Old Testament, was based on laws and regulations handed down through Moses, but it did not provide for a direct access and relationship with God.

- The New Covenant is based on God's Grace, Love and Mercy through the shed Blood of Jesus His Son on the cross, and it does provide for direct access to God and leadership of the indwelling Holy Spirit.

How did the New Covenant come into being?
The Plan of the Ages

- God knew before the foundation of the earth that man would fall into sin and break relationship with Him.

So, the all-knowing God provided a way for the mankind He loved (us/you) to spend eternity with Him in Heaven. His Son Jesus, would have to be the once and for all sacrifice. Jesus was willing to be that sacrifice.

- Through His prophets of Old, God had stated more than 300 times that this New Covenant was coming through the promised Messiah (God's Son).

- No matter what walk of life or what religious background we have come from, we can only come to God through Jesus, His Son. We are instructed by Jesus Himself, that we must live under the New Covenant.

- During the night of the Last Supper, Jesus discussed this New Covenant and said, that the Holy Spirit would bring it to (His Bride) His church. Jesus was transitioning His disciples from The Law to Grace. John chapters 15-17 and Hebrews chapters 7-9.

- The next morning, Jesus paid the MAXIMUM PRICE, to give us the New Covenant.

- Fifty days after Jesus was resurrected, the Holy Spirit ushered in the New Covenant on the day of Pentecost. This was foreshadowed with the Israelites on their first Pentecost, fifty days after they were led out of Egypt by Moses.

Why do we need the New Covenant with God?

- We need the New Covenant so that we may have direct access and fellowship with God and to receive God's blessings and leadership.

- The New Covenant gives us the Guidelines to live by and the instructions on how to have that close relationship with our Heavenly Father.

- Being Born-Again is having your spirit recreated so that you can have that person-to-person relationship with God.

- Now that Jesus is your personal Savior, you have become the bride of Christ and a joint heir with Him.

HEBREWS 7:15-28 AND 8:1-2

15. So we can plainly see that God's method changed, for Christ, the NEW High Priest who came with the rank of Melchizedek,
16. did not become a priest by meeting the old requirement of belonging to the tribe of Levi, but on the basis of POWER FLOWING FROM A LIFE THAT CANNOT END.
17. And the Psalmist points this out when He says of Christ, "You are a PRIEST FOREVER WITH THE RANK OF MELCHIZEDEK."
18. Yes, the old system of priesthood based on family lines was canceled because it didn't work. It was weak and useless for saving people.
19. It never made anyone really right with God. But now we have a far better hope, FOR CHRIST MAKES US ACCEPTABLE TO GOD, AND NOW WE MAY DRAW NEAR TO HIM.
20. God took an oath that Christ would always be a Priest,
21. although He never said that of other priests. Only to Christ He said, "The Lord has sworn and will never change His mind: YOU ARE A PRIEST FOREVER, WITH THE RANK OF MELCHIZEDEK."
22. Because of God's oath, CHRIST CAN GUARANTEE FOREVER THE SUCCESS OF THIS NEW AND BETTER ARRANGEMENT.
23. Under the old arrangement there had to be many priests, so that when the older ones died off, the system could still be carried on by others who took their places.
24. BUT JESUS LIVES FOREVER AND CONTINUES TO BE A PRIEST SO THAT NO ONE ELSE IS NEEDED.
25. He is able to save completely all who come to God through Him. Since He will live forever, He will always be there to remind God that He has paid for their sins with His blood.
26. He is, therefore, exactly the kind of High Priest we need, for He is holy and blameless, unstained by sin, undefiled by sinners, and to Him has been given the PLACE of HONOR IN HEAVEN.
27. He never needs the daily blood of animal sacrifices, as other priests did, to cover over first their own sins and then the sins of the people; for HE FINISHED ALL SACRIFICES, ONCE AND FOR ALL, WHEN HE SACRIFICED HIMSELF ON THE CROSS.
28. Under the old system, even the high priests were weak and sinful men who could not keep from doing wrong, BUT LATER GOD APPOINTED BY HIS OATH HIS SON WHO IS PERFECT FOREVER.

8:1-2 What we are saying is this: CHRIST, WHOSE PRIEST HOOD WE HAVE JUST DESCRIBED, IS OUR HIGH PRIEST, AND IS IN HEAVEN AT THE PLACE OF GREATEST HONOR NEXT TO GOD HIMSELF. HE MINISTERS IN THE TEMPLE IN HEAVEN, THE TRUE PLACE OF WORSHIP BUILT BY THE LORD AND NOT BY HUMAN HANDS.

Scripture quotations are taken from *The Living Bible, copyright 1971.*
Used by permission of Tyndale House Publishers, Inc.
Wheaton, IL 60189 USA. All rights reserved.

THE NIGHT OF THE LAST SUPPER
WITH JESUS' FINAL EXHORTATION
AND INTRODUCTION TO THE NEW COVENANT

It was customary in Old Testament days when a person was aware that God was going to take him home, he normally called in his family and the person he had been training to take his place and gave them blessings and words of final exhortation.

Jesus was no exception. He knew very well that His time had come. So He made arrangements for the Passover meal. Jesus wanted a quiet place so there would be no interruptions with the few short hours He had with the ones He loved.

In his gospel, John describes what happened on this special evening with Jesus. We will look at Chapters 12-18. Let's pray that the Holy Spirit will give us revelation concerning the things Jesus did and said and how it applies to us today.

Jesus, in principal, laid the Father's HEART on the table and said, THIS IS HOW MUCH THE FATHER LOVES YOU, AND THIS IS HIS PROVISION AND THE RESOURCES HE HAS MADE AVAILABLE TO YOU THAT YOU MAY HAVE LIFE AND LIFE MORE ABUNDANTLY.

The New Covenant Jesus made reference to has a time span of TWO THOUSAND YEARS (also Matthew 26:28). The person of the Holy Spirit ushered in this NEW COVENANT from the Father on the Day of Pentecost, and it is VALID UNTIL THE RAPTURE occurs (II Thessalonians 2:1).

This covenant is in FULL FORCE TODAY. Everything we read about in the New Testament applies to us on every issue. There is no scriptural evidence that there would be ANY CHANGES in God's COVENANT. We are told in Galatians 3:13-14 that the promises of Abraham apply to us also. This covenant applies after we have received Jesus as Savior and have been BORN-AGAIN. In Revelation 22:19 we read that no one should add or take away from what God has established by His Word.

In Hebrews we read "GOD REWARDS THEM THAT DILIGENTLY SEEK HIM." With this verse in mind, we want to encourage and challenge you to "Grow in GRACE and in the KNOWLEDGE of our Lord and Savior Jesus Christ. To Him be glory both now and forever. Amen". II Peter 3:18

We will highlight John beginning with Chapter 12, which begins six days before the crucifixion. Jesus and the disciples had dinner with Martha, Mary, and Lazarus (the Lazarus Jesus had raised from the dead).

At this time Mary took a bottle of ointment and poured it on Jesus' feet, and then she wiped His feet with her hair. Judas made a comment about Mary being wasteful, that this expensive ointment should have been sold and the money given to the poor.

THE NIGHT OF THE LAST SUPPER Page 2

Jesus took this opportunity to start preparing His disciples for His death that was only a few days away.

The next day is the day we know as Palm Sunday. Many people had come to town for the feast. They had heard that Jesus was there. This is when Jesus fulfilled one of the many prophecies about the coming Messiah: "The Messiah would ride into town on a young donkey."

More people came looking for Jesus. He again spoke about his coming death, using the parable "Except a corn of wheat fall into the ground." This is in reference to the necessity of His sacrifice, which includes the death, the burial, and the resurrection.

The next time Jesus spoke He said, "I have not come to judge the world but that through Me the world might be saved." He also stated He was the light of the world and whosoever received Him would receive eternal life.

Chapter 13 brings us to the day of the Passover feast (Luke 22:8-13). Jesus sends Peter and John to make arrangements for the Passover meal in the upper room. Jesus knew His hour had come.

After supper, He begins to exhort and teach the disciples. He begins with washing their feet and explaining if they are not cleansed God's way they cannot have a part in the Kingdom of Heaven. Jesus gave an example to us that we should serve one another (John 13:2-17).

Verse 20 of John 13 is the first reference Jesus gives to Him sending the Holy Spirit to take His place.

Then He speaks of the one that is going to betray Him in verse 21. Jesus identifies Judas as that person. Then He sends Judas out to do what he must do in verses 18-30.

In verses 31-33 Jesus begins the final exhortation, "Now is the Son of man glorified, and God is glorified in Him. A NEW COMMANDMENT I give unto you: That you LOVE one another, AS I HAVE LOVED YOU."

Then Peter said in verse 36, "Lord, where are you going, and can I follow you?" Jesus' answer was, "Where I am going you can't follow me now, but you shall follow me at a later time." Then Jesus told Peter, "Tonight you will deny me three times before the cock crows."

Jesus changes the tone of what He has been saying in Chapter 14. He starts to comfort them by saying, "Don't worry. I am going home, and when I get home I am going to prepare a place for you. Then I will come back for you."

In verse 4, Thomas asked a very important question, "Where are you going and how can we follow?"

THE NIGHT OF THE LAST SUPPER Page 3

The answer Jesus gave in verses 6-7 is also very important. Jesus said, "I am the WAY, the TRUTH, and the LIFE; no man can come to the Father except by me."

Then Philip asked in verse 8, "Lord, show us the Father." Jesus answered in verses 9-11, "Philip, you have been with me for three years. Everything you have seen me do has been directed by the Father. I do not do anything apart from Him. He lives in Me, and I live in Him. The Father will live in you the same way He lives in Me."

Jesus presents a NEW CONCEPT of prayer and relationship with the Father in verses 12-15. He said, "If we BELIEVE on Him, LOVE Him, and OBEY His commandments, we can ask the Father anything in Jesus Name, and our Father will do it."

Here again in verses 16-26, Jesus is talking about the person of the Holy Spirit. Jesus said He would ask the Father, and the FATHER would give you another comforter. The NEW comforter shall be with you and shall be IN you. Verse 19 says the world will not see Jesus any more, but through the indwelling Holy Spirit we will know and see Jesus. BECAUSE JESUS LIVES we will live also.

To recap verses 20-26, Jesus said, "AT THAT DAY." He was referring to the day of Pentecost and the coming of the Holy Spirit to indwell the believers. The Holy Spirit will work from the inside out (Paul said, "the inner man") to give revelation (Rhema) concerning who God is and who Jesus is. And through the revelation power of the Holy Spirit, we can understand that THEY INDWELL us, and our body HAS become THE TEMPLE OF THE HOLY SPIRIT.

If we obey His commandments, the Holy Spirit will teach us all things.

Again in verses 27-31 Jesus comforts the disciples. Their hearts must be hurting and their heads reeling from what Jesus has been saying to them. Now He says, "Peace I leave with you, not the peace the world has to offer but MY divine peace." (See THE FRUIT OF THE SPIRIT, Lesson 9)

Jesus goes on to say, "After tonight I will not talk to you much, but I am telling you these things before they come to pass, and as the Father has told ME things to do, I am telling YOU things to do."

In chapter 15 Jesus has taken the disciples out from the table setting, and now they are walking toward the Garden of Gethsemane. As they walk and as Jesus talks, they can look at the things around them, and what Jesus is saying will have a greater impact on their mind and heart.

Beginning in verse 1 Jesus says, "I AM the vine, and my Father is the husbandman." We (you) are the branches Jesus points out, and apart from Him, we cannot do anything on behalf of the kingdom.

THE NIGHT OF THE LAST SUPPER Page 4

THE FATHER IS GLORIFIED IF WE BEAR MUCH FRUIT, verse 8.

Jesus goes on to say in verses 9-16, "As the Father has loved Me, so I HAVE LOVED YOU; continue in my love so that MY JOY will be in you, and that your joy might be full, I command you to love one another. You did not choose me, I chose you, and I ordained you to go forth and be fruitful, and that whatever you ask in my Name, the Father will do it."

When the Holy Spirit comes, He shall testify of Jesus Christ, using (us) the body of Christ as His team. Verses 26-27:

Jesus and the disciples are still walking as we enter chapter 16. He is saying to them in verses 1-4, "I am telling you these things in advance so you don't get your feelings hurt when people do bad things to you because you are being obedient to what I have told you to do." (Saul persecuted the church in the Book Of Acts.)

"You haven't asked where I am going; sorrow has filled your heart" (verses 5-6).

In verses 7-15 Jesus picks up again the importance and the necessity about the person of the Holy Spirit coming to take up where Jesus left off. In these verses He mentions the Holy Spirit fourteen times to make His point. Then Jesus goes on to say, "There is more I want to teach you, but you could not digest it at this time. However, when the Holy Spirit comes, He will teach you all things."

"In a little while you will not see me (referring to three days in the grave), and then you shall see me. You will have sorrow for a short time, and the world will be rejoicing, but then when you see me again, you will be rejoicing for evermore" (verses 16-22).

"In that day" (verses 23-28) references from, the day of Pentecost to the Rapture (about 2000 years). The New Covenant has been brought in by the Holy Spirit. We have been instructed by Jesus to ask the Father for our needs in Jesus' name. For the disciples, this was a new concept in regard to receiving from God, who has now become, their and our Heavenly Father. Before this, under the Old Covenant, they went to the Priest and he would petition God on their behalf. (John 16:22-28)

Jesus continues to speak, "You are going to be scattered for a moment, but I will gather you together again. I want you to have PEACE. CHEER UP! I HAVE OVERCOME THE WORLD", verses 32-33.

After speaking all these things to the disciples, Jesus began to speak to the Father. In Chapter 17 we have what is referred to as the HIGH PRIESTLY PRAYER. In this prayer Jesus makes four petitions to the Father.

In verses 1-5 Jesus prays for His **Glorification**.

THE NIGHT OF THE LAST SUPPER Page 5

In verses 6-16 Jesus prays for the **preservation of the disciples**, and He asks the Father to protect them because they did not belong to the world.

The third petition is in John 17:17-20. Jesus prayed for **the sanctification of the church** and said, "Father as you have sent me, I am sending the church. Father I pray for the future believers." JESUS COMMITTED HIMSELF FOR OUR GROWTH TODAY.

In verses 19-26 Jesus is praying the most important forth petition, **that ALL BELIEVERS would be ONE, AS HE AND THE FATHER ARE ONE.** Jesus wants us to understand that the Father loves us, as much as HE LOVES HIS only BEGOTTEN SON.

Now as we move into chapter 18:1, Jesus takes the disciples over the brook into the garden.

Verse 2 tells us that Judas knew where Jesus would be.

When Judas and the religious leaders along with the soldiers
(reported to be about 600 total people) came to them, Jesus asked, "Who are you looking for?" At those words, they all fell flat on their backs. This shows they could not take Jesus by force, but He gave Himself willingly.

The rest of the night and morning were spent in trials before the Jews and Pilate.

In Chapter 19:1 Jesus is taken by the soldiers and scourged. This fulfills prophecy where it says, "By His stripes we are healed."

Then Jesus, the Son of God, was crucified, AND THE MOST EXCITING PART OF THIS STORY IS:

ON THE FIRST DAY OF THE WEEK

JESUS AROSE FROM THE GRAVE.

HE BROKE THE POWER

OVER

SIN AND DEATH !

THE FOUR STAGES OF SPIRITUAL GROWTH

II Peter 3:18: GROW IN GRACE AND IN THE KNOWLEDGE OF OUR LORD AND SAVIOUR JESUS CHRIST. The scriptures reveal four stages of spiritual growth in the Christian life.

1. **The Baby Stage** - I Corinthians 3:1-4

    A baby thinks only of self, and if denied the things desired, it will raise a rumpus. It seeks its own; its feelings are easily hurt, and it is often jealous. A baby lives to be served--it never serves. It drinks milk and cannot eat strong meat. It cries but never sings. It tries to talk, but never makes sense. These infant characteristics are so prominent in the lives of many church members. They have been born into the family of God but have failed to develop spiritually. They are spiritual babies--carnal Christians.

2. **The Little Child Stage** - I John 2:12

    Some Christians grow to be little children spiritually but stop there. Here are some of the characteristics of children: They are often untruthful, envious, and cruel. If rebuked, they become martyrs; if crossed, they are resentful and often make a scene. They are talebearers, repeating everything they hear.
    (IN ADULTS IT IS CALLED GOSSIP) They are given to emotional outbursts and are easily puffed up. They love praise and will accept it from any source. They seek only the things that appeal to self.
    ARE YOU A SPIRITUAL CHILD?

3. **The Young Man Stage** - I John 2:13

    Spiritual growth to that of a young man, is not reached by many. He is strong and virile and is well able to overcome his enemy. He has a vision for the future and the faith and courage to tackle it. He is preparing for his productive years. You, too, can become a young man spiritually by putting away childish things, AND GROW (I Corinthians 13:11).

4. **The Father Stage** - I John 2:13

    All can reach this stage of spiritual development, but so few ever attain it. The spiritual father has peace with God (Romans 5:1). He knows the peace of God (Philippians 4:7). He rejoices in his spiritual children.
    (I Thessalonians 2:19 and Timothy 1:2) He has learned contentment under all circumstances (Philippians 4:11). He knows the only source of true strength (Philippians 4:13). HE DOES NOT BROOD OVER THE PAST but looks to the future (Philippians 3:13-14). He knows that all things work together in his life for his eternal good (Romans 8:28). He enjoys the abundant life now and will enjoy it in the life to come (Ephesians 2:7).

NOTE: From, *The Christian Life New Testament.* Copyright 1978, 1969, 1967 by Royal Publishers. Used by permission of Thomas Nelson, Inc.

IN HIM

In lesson one we mentioned that under the New Covenant, a child of God has an indescribable Benefit Package. We want to give you a partial list of scripture to reinforce who you are and what you have in Jesus, God's Son.

IN CHRIST

Rom. 3:24	Gal. 2:4	Col. 1:28
Rom. 8:1	Gal. 3:26	1 Thes. 4:16
Rom. 8:2	Gal. 3:28	1 Thes. 5:18
Rom. 12:5	Gal. 5:6	1 Tim. 1:14
1 Cor. 1:2	Gal. 6:15	2 Tim. 1:9
1 Cor. 1:30	Eph. 1:3	2 Tim. 1:13
1 Cor. 15:22	Eph. 1:10	2 Tim. 2:1
2 Cor. 1:21	Eph. 2:6	2 Tim 2:10
2 Cor. 2:14	Eph. 2:10	2 Tim. 3:15
2 Cor. 3:14	Eph. 2:13	Phile. 1:6
2 Cor. 5:17	Eph. 3:6	2 Peter 1:8
2 Cor. 5:19	Phil. 3:13,14	
2 John 1:9		

BY HIMSELF
Heb. 1:3   Heb. 9:26

BY HIS BLOOD
Heb. 9:11,12   Heb. 10:19,20
1 John 1:7   Heb. 9:14,15

BY WHOM
Rom. 5:2   Rom. 5:11   Gal. 6:14

FROM WHOM
Eph. 4:16   Col. 2:19

OF CHRIST
2 Cor. 2:5   Col. 2:17   Col. 3:24
Phil. 3:12

OF HIM
1 John 1:5   1 John 2:27

THROUGH HIM
John 3:17   Rom. 8:37   1 John 4:9
Rom. 5:9

THROUGH CHRIST

Rom. 5:1	1 Cor. 15:57	Phil. 4:6-7
Rom. 5:11	Gal. 3:13-14	Phil. 4:13
Rom. 6:11	Gal. 4:7	Heb. 10:10
Rom. 6:23	Eph. 2:7	Heb. 13:20-21

WITH CHRIST

Rom. 6:8	Eph. 2:5	Col. 3:1
Gal. 2:20	Col. 2:20	Col. 3:3

IN HIM

Acts 17:28	Col. 2:6	1 John 3:3
John 1:4	Col. 2:7	1 John 3:5
John 3:15,16	Col. 2:10	1 John 3:6
2 Cor. 1:20	1 John 2:5	1 John 3:24
2 Cor. 5:21	1 John 2:6	1 John 4:13
Eph. 1:4	1 John 2:8	1 John 5:14,15
Eph. 1:10	1 John 2:27	1 John 5:20
Phil. 3:9	1 John 2:28	

IN WHOM

Eph. 1:7	Eph. 2:21	Col. 1:14
Eph. 1:11	Eph. 2:22	Col. 2:3
Eph. 1:13	Eph. 3:12	Col. 2:11
1 Pet. 1:8		

BY HIM

1 Cor. 1:5	Col. 1:17	Heb. 7:25
1 Cor. 8:6	Col. 1:20	Heb. 13:15
Col. 1:16	Col. 3:17	1 Pet. 1:21

WITH HIM

Rom. 6:4	Rom. 8:32	Col. 2:13-15
Rom. 6:6	2 Cor. 13:4	Col. 3:4
Rom. 6:8	Col. 2:12	2 Tim. 2:11

LESSON – 2

LEARNING HOW TO STUDY GOD'S WORD

THE BIBLE

IS THE WORD OF GOD

AND

IT IS THE TIP OF THE

ICEBERG

OF ALL GOD HAS TO OFFER

AND

IT WILL SINK

THE

LEARNING HOW TO STUDY GOD'S WORD

INTRODUCTION

Stages of learning move in three particular ways. The order cannot be reversed for God has made people TO operate in this way.

- a. Intellect - Analyzes the facts and tries to understand.
- b. Emotion - Responds to the principle drawn from the facts.
- c. Will - Takes the principle and applies it to life so changes are made.

1. HOW WE HEAR AND READ THE WORD AND APPLY IT TO OUR LIVES IS OF PRIME IMPORTANCE. Matthew 13:3-23

The parable of the sower describes four different responses to the Word.

- a. The Way Side - Fowl devoured the seed.
- b. Stony Place - No root; the seed withered away.
- c. Thorns - Choked the seed.
- d. Good Ground - Brought forth fruit.

NOTE: The natural man cannot understand the spiritual meaning of the parable. The hidden meaning was for those whose hearts were open to the truth. (I Corinthians 2:14 and 14:23). THE SEED REPRESENTS THE WORD OF GOD AND THE GROUND REPRESENTS OUR HEARTS.

RESPONSES TO THE WORD

- a. The Way Side - "I don't understand." This person never puts a guard around the Word, never prays, and allows the enemy to snatch it away.
- b. Stony Place - This experience usually was one of emotion, and when the trials of life came there was no sound footing to stand firm upon.
- c. Thorns - The cares of the world, deceitfulness of riches, pleasures, no time for the Lord--all choked out the Word.
- d. Good Ground - Hears, understands, responds, and allows the seed to take root and grow so it can produce fruit. (GOD CAN TILL YOUR SOIL)

MEMORY VERSES (Also, look at the Faith Helps in the back of the manual)

Matthew 6:33	Seek ye first.
II Timothy 2:15	Study to show.
Romans 12:2	Be ye transformed.
Joshua 1:8	Meditate on the Word.
John 16:12-14	Jesus wants you to keep growing.

LEARNING HOW TO STUDY GOD'S WORD

2. **MEDITATING ON THE WORD IS IMPORTANT**

   It is important to turn scripture over in your mind and chew it like a cow chews its cud. WHY? Because it is a message from God, and each word has a significance and truth in it that He wants you to know.
   (It is Sifting God's Word From The Head To The Heart, page 20)

   Let the words of my mouth and the meditation of my heart be acceptable in thy sight, O Lord, my strength and my redeemer
   (Psalm 19:14).

   Thy Word have I hid in mine heart, that I might not sin against thee.
   (Psalm 119:11 also Joshua 1:8 - Be a success).

3. **MEMORIZATION OF THE WORD IS IMPORTANT**

   When you memorize the scripture you show God that you mean business, that your salvation is not just a passing fad.

   You need to have a ready resource of scripture inside of you to combat the enemy. Jesus said, "It is written" (Luke 4:1-14).

   Knowing the Word makes you an effective witness for your Lord.
   (Acts 8:26-35)

4. **APPLICATION OF THE WORD TO OUR LIFE IS IMPORTANT**

   Pastors, evangelists, teachers, and other Christians may be a great influence and a great help to you, but the most effective voice speaking to your heart is the Holy Spirit.

   Whatever the source, it is only effective in your life if you apply the truths that are revealed to you (James 1:21-22).

   Mary sat at the feet of Jesus. He said, "She hath CHOSEN that good part which shall not be taken from her" (Luke 10:38).

5. **THE METHOD THAT GOD HAS CHOSEN TO TEACH YOU IS HIS WORD**

   Establish your confidence and dependence on the Bible as being God's direct instructions to you, **HIS WORD THAT HE WANTS YOU TO FOLLOW.**

   GOD'S WORD DOES NOT RETURN TO HIM VOID, BUT IT **ACCOMPLISHES** WHATEVER HE SENT IT TO DO (Isaiah 55:11).

LEARNING HOW TO STUDY GOD'S WORD
- REVIEW -

1. Name the three stages of learning in order.

    a.

    b.

    c.

2. In the Parable of the Sower (Matthew 13:3-23), what four types of ground are mentioned, and what does the seed represent?

    a.   d.

    b.   e.

    c.

3. When you have difficulty understanding the Bible, what should you do? Scripture please.

4. Name the FOUR IMPORTANT THINGS we should remember about being grounded in the Word.

    a.

    b.

    c.

    d.

5. Whose voice should you listen to more than any other when you are seeking to apply the Word to your life?

6. What method has God chosen to teach you His ways?

SO HOW DO WE STUDY THE BIBLE?
Page 1

1. Find a place that is quiet and allow adequate time to study several times a week.

2. Pray before, during, and after your Bible study, asking God to open your heart to His Word.

3. Use a Bible that you enjoy reading and have a notebook, pen, highlighter, etc.

4. Read the New Testament through at least seven times beginning at the Gospel of John. Bypass the Book of Revelation because it can sidetrack you from your GOAL at this time.

5. Then start reading one book of the Old Testament (starting at Genesis) and then back to the New Testament. Start reading the Gospel of Matthew this time.

6. As you read, ask yourself the following questions.

   a. What does this chapter say about Jesus?

   b. What does this chapter say about the Holy Spirit?

   c. Who is this chapter talking to?

   - The Jews
   - The Nation of Israel
   - The Gentiles
   - The Church
   - You / Me

   d. How does this chapter apply to me today?

   e. What did God say about this subject?

   f. What did Jesus say about this subject?

   g. What did the disciples say about this subject?

SO HOW DO WE STUDY THE BIBLE?
Page 2

7. Write down the questions you have and the questions that come up as you read in your notebook and date them. Then when you get the answers, write them down and date them too. You will see God is working with you to help you to understand His Word.
The Bible will answer your questions.

8. Make notes in your Bible. Underline verses that stand out to you.

9. You may use other references such as, a Strong's Concordance, or a topical study explaining the customs during Bible times.

10. Start a Topical Chain Reference in your Bible going from verse to verse. Use verses that say the same thing so you can develop the Seven Sets of Scripture practice.
    Some Topic Examples are;
    a. The first coming of Jesus
    b. The second coming of Jesus
    c. The Holy Spirit
    d. Water baptism

11. Find three to seven sets of scripture on the subject you are working on. This is how you can make the adjustments in your life that are necessary, to line up with God's Word. Look at the In Him verses on page 14 and the Faith Helps, in the back of this manual.

12. Do not try to interpret the Bible. Let scripture speak to you the way it is written in your Bible. Stay away from the one-half verse or the one-verse method of trying to prove a point. God did not give instructions on how to interpret His Word. He only gave instructions on, HOW TO OBEDIENTLY FOLLOW HIS WORD AND HOW TO BE LED BY THE HOLY SPIRIT.

Do these exercises when you are reading, or studying, and after each lesson. Using this method purifies the Word in your heart. MAY YOU GROW IN GRACE AND IN THE KNOWLEDGE OF YOUR LORD AND SAVIOR JESUS CHRIST.

HOW TO SIFT GOD'S WORD
FROM THE HEAD TO THE HEART

REMEMBER; The Bible separates the head from the heart.

1. **Review;** The FOUR STAGES OF CHRISTIAN GROWTH

    a. Review the four types of soil (Matthew 13:1-23).
    b. Man shall not live by bread alone (Matthew 4:4).
    c. Heaven and earth shall pass away, but My Word will last forever.

2. **Review;** THE NIGHT OF THE LAST SUPPER and EXAMINE THE NEW COVENANT. Jesus sent the Holy Spirit to initiate our spiritual growth.

3. God's basic principal **IS**, EVERYTHING He **has** for us, **is received by faith**. Faith comes by hearing the Word of God. (Romans 10:9-10). Without faith it is impossible to please God (Hebrews 11:6). We receive by faith in the heart, not knowledge in the head. This is why we must learn, to get into God's Word first, so we can pray from the heart, in faith. An example of Rhema in the inner man, is in Ephesians 1:17-23, 2:1 and 3:16-20.

4. STUDY God's word (II Timothy 2:15) and grow in grace and knowledge. (II Peter 3:18). The Bible is the Holy Spirit's toolbox.

5. MEMORIZE God's Word. Psalm 119:11 says, "I hide your word in my heart." Also Proverbs 3:5-7.

6. MEDITATE on God's Word (Joshua 1:8).

7. Then SPEAK God's Word (Romans 10:9-10).

8. PRAY--before, during, and after reading God's word. Matthew 7:7-8,ask, seek, knock. Also Jeremiah 33:3, call on God.

9. Start a daily DEVOTION TIME (Proverbs 8:17).

10. There is only one way to commit God's Word to memory,
    --REVIEW- REVIEW- REVIEW--.
    Your eyes, ears, and mind are the gate to your heart. (The inner man)

11. My people are destroyed for lack of knowledge (Hosea 4:6).

12. Without a vision my people perish (Proverbs 29:18).

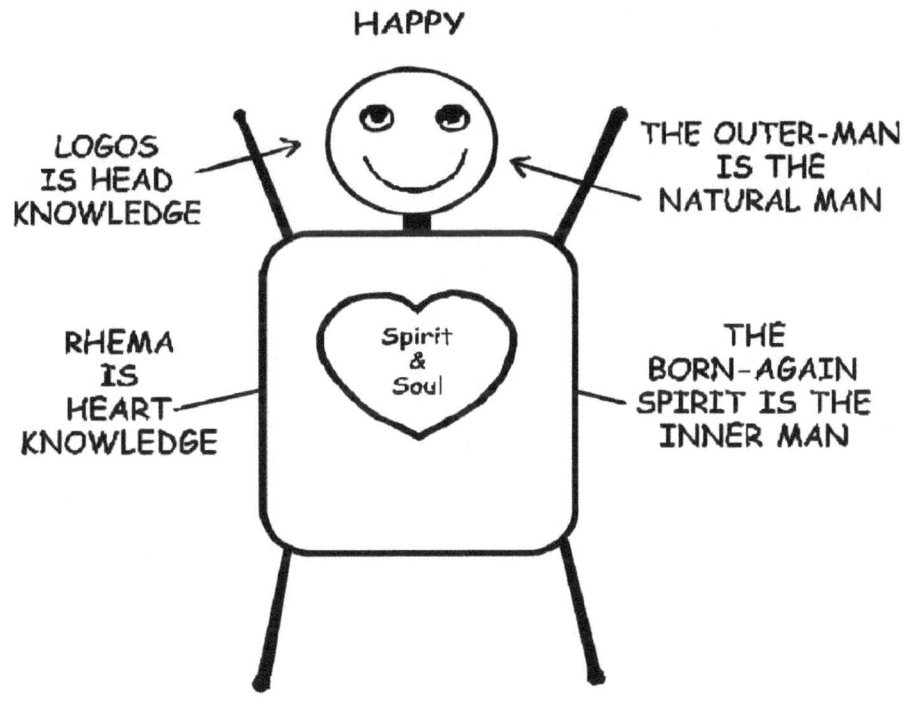

THE BIBLE SEPERATES THE NATURAL MAN FROM THE SPIRITUAL MAN. EPHESIANS 1:17-23 & EPHESIANS 3:16-20

THROUGH THE FOUR STAGES OF GROWTH, THE INNER MAN BECOMES STRONG ENOUGH TO TAKE CONTROL OVER THE NATURAL MAN AND STOPS HIM FROM SINNING.
2 CORINTHIANS 10:4-6 AND GALATIANS, CHAPTER 5

THE SPIRITUAL MAN LEARNING TO BE LED BY THE HOLY SPIRIT IS WHAT PAUL IS TALKING ABOUT WHEN HE SAYS, "WORK OUT YOUR OWN SALVATION." LESSON 11

GOD'S WORD APPLIED WILL WEAVE THE FABRIC OF FAITH INTO YOUR INNER SPIRIT. 2 PETER 3:18

GOD'S WORD APPLIED

The Holy Spirit works in our inner man in conjunction with *God's WORD* and our response and obedience to it. James 1:22 says, "Be ye a doer of the *WORD* and not a hearer only". This is the *APPLICATION* of the *WORD*, to our heart and life, and where the child-like faith is developed.

You are *CLEANSED* by the *WORD*, John 15:3.

You are, *TRANSFORMED,* by the *WORD*, Romans 12:1-2.

FAITH, comes by hearing, and hearing by the *WORD* of God", Romans 10:17.

The *WORD* is near you, in your mouth and in your heart, Romans 10:8-10.

You are a *SUCCESS* through the *WORD*, Joshua 1:8.

"If you abide in Me, and *My WORDS* (RHEMA) abide in you, you shall ask what you will, and it will be done for you", John 15:7.

You are *MAINTAINED* through the *WORD*. David said; "I hide Your *WORD* in my heart, so I will not sin against You", Psalms 119:11.

Jesus said, "The Holy Spirit will bring, ALL THINGS, (*My WORD*) I taught you, to remembrance", John 16:12.

"Heaven and earth shall pass away, but My *WORD* will live forever", Matthew 24:35.

The Lord knows the thoughts and intentions of the heart, Hebrews 4:12.

LESSON - 3

LEARNING HOW TO PRAY

BECAUSE OF GOD'S

DIVERSITY

WE MUST BE FLEXIBLE

OR

WE WILL MISS OUT

ON

WHAT GOD IS DOING

I Corinthians 12:1-13

Now there are DIVERSITIES of Gifts,
but the SAME SPIRIT,
And
There are DIVERSITIES of ADMINISTRATION
BUT THE SAME Lord
And
There are DIVERSITIES of OPERATIONS
But it is the SAME GOD WHICH WORKETH ALL IN ALL.

LEARNING HOW TO PRAY

1. **WHAT HAVE WE LEARNED IN LESSONS ONE AND TWO?**
   We learned, that we are NOT GOD'S after thought, we were HIS first thought, HIS PRIORITY.

2. The GOD HEAD, COUNTED THE COST BEFORE the FOUNDATION OF THE EARTH. Jesus **KNEW** He had to *DIE ON THE CROSS*, BEFORE the earth was created. Jesus was *OBEDIENT* to the Father to PAY THE PRICE OF SIN, so the Father could have a people that *LOVE HIM* and would be able to live FOREVER with the *FATHER* in heaven. This same people would also be the **BRIDE OF CHRIST**.

3. Paul reviewed the Gospel in I Corinthians Ch. 15, how the Old Testament Scriptures prophesied the first coming of the Messiah and *THE SUPREME SACRIFICE HE* would pay at *THE CRUCIFIXION, THE BURIAL AND THE RESURRECTION*. There are more than three hundred *PROPHECIES* concerning the *FIRST* coming of Jesus in the Old Testament.

4. *THE GOD HEAD HAS COME TO LIVE IN YOU.* If you are *BORN-AGAIN*, you have become the *TEMPLE OF GOD*.

5. You have become THE BRIDE OF GOD'S SON AND A JOINT HEIR WITH HIM. As BRIDE AND GROOM we became ONE WITH HIM.

6. Jesus has given us, (THE BORN-AGAIN CHURCH) all of the RESOURCES HE HAD while He was here on earth in His human body.

7. JESUS – THE GOD MAN – THE SON OF GOD, LEFT EVERY-THING IN HEAVEN WHEN HE CAME TO EARTH TO BE BORN OF A VIRGIN.

8. When Jesus left heaven to be born of a virgin, He left every-thing that He had, EXCEPT for what He intended to leave His bride when He returned to Heaven.

9. The only advantage Jesus had over us *IS* His relationship with His Father. This relationship included,

   - *THE POWER OF THE HOLY SPIRIT*
   - *THE GIFTS OF THE HOLY SPIRIT*
   - *THE FRUIT OF THE HOLY SPIRIT*
   - *ALONG WITH KNOWING WHO HE IS*
   - *WHOSE HE IS, AND WHERE HE WAS FROM*
   - *WHAT HIS MISSION WAS*
   - *AND WHERE HE WAS GOING BACK TOO.*

ALL OF THIS RELATIONSHIP PACKAGE BELONGS TO YOU NOW, AS JESUS' BRIDE.

LEARNING HOW TO PRAY
Page 2

10. When Jesus said to the disciples, " **Wait for the PROMISE OF THE FATHER**", He was telling them to wait for the Holy Spirit to **bring His Bride the NEW COVENANT PACKAGE**, WHICH HAS, EVERY-THING YOU NEED, TO BE WHAT JESUS WANTS YOU TO BE.

11. Jesus paid the **PRICE for our COMPLETE REDEMPTION, SPIRIT, SOUL AND BODY.** This should be thoroughly understood in the inner spirit in order for us to pray in faith, expecting results to our prayers and to live our daily life that is pleasing to our Lord.

12. **TIME AND DISTANCE HAVE NO IMPACT ON YOUR PRAYER POWER. (Romans 8:28-29)**

13. We have learned that our **SPIRITUAL GROWTH IS PROGRESSIVE THROUGH the WRITTEN WORD** and with the **application** of *THE WORD* and **WITH THE HELP OF THE HOLY SPIRIT.** *We CAN GROW,* TO THE SPIRITUAL LEVEL OUR FATHER WOULD LIKE US TO GROW TOO. PRAYER IS THE DOOR TO THE RELATIONSHIP WITH OUR FATHER THAT JESUS HAS.

    WE NOW HAVE DIRECT ACCESS TO THE THRONE OF GOD.
    Hebrews 4:14-16

JESUS CAME TO SET THE CAPTIVES FREE

Jesus delivered us . . . . Colossians 1:13-20

Jesus Full of the Holy Spirit . . Luke 4:1, Acts 10:38 & John Ch. 17

Jesus returned to Galilee . . . . . Luke 4:14-21

The Lord's desired fast . . . . . . Isaiah 58:6-11

**For God so *LOVED* the world
that He *GAVE* His only *BEGOTTEN SON*...
John 3:16.**

LEARNING HOW TO PRAY
Page 3

A natural father talks to his baby before that baby can respond or talk back.

Our Heavenly Father did this for us in the Bible. While we were yet sinners, He had a message of love for us. (The Plan of the Ages)

Now as His children we have the great privilege of talking to Him and having Him hear and answer our prayers.

1. **WHAT IS PRAYER?**

    a. PRAYER is SIMPLY TALKING to your Heavenly Father.

    b. PRAYER is THE SOURCE for all of our needs to be met, including a release from tensions and anxieties, etc. I Peter 5:7 says to cast ALL OF OUR CARE UPON HIM. Luke 1:37: "For with God nothing shall be impossible."

    c. PRAYER is the DOORWAY to a successful Christian life. In Luke 11:11-13 Jesus is telling us the Father wants us to ask for our needs. In Ephesians 3:20 God promises He is able to do exceeding abundantly above ALL THAT WE ASK OR THINK.

    d. PRAYER MOTIVATES to success. As you wait in His presence, your goals become crystal clear, and the power to successfully reach those goals is bestowed upon you.

    e. CREATIVE ANSWERS to your problems are found in prayer.

    f. PRAYER SHUTS OUT the world (Matthew 6:6).

    g. PRAYER will bring about changes that are needed in your life. There are some things that will never happen unless you pray.

    IT IS YOUR RESPONSIBILITY TO MAKE YOUR NEEDS KNOWN TO THE FATHER. It is part of His plan that certain things don't take place until men pray.

2. **DIFFERENT TYPES OF PRAYER**

    a. **WORSHIP:** If any man be a worshiper of God and does His will, the Father will HEAR him (John 4:21-24 & 9:31).
    b. **CONFESSION:** If we confess our sins, He forgives us, (I John 1:9).
    c. **SUPPLICATION:** For all men (I Timothy 2:1).
    d. **INTERCESSION:** Jesus teaches us how to pray (John 17:1-26).
    e. **IMPORTUNE:** Ask, seek, and find (Luke 11:5-10).

    f. Refer to TYPES OF PRAYER in this lesson.

LEARNING HOW TO PRAY
Page 4

3. **BASIS OF ANSWERED PRAYER**

   a. Your prayers are answered when you OBEY God. When you are right with God, your prayers make the greatest things in life available.
      (I John 1:9 and 3:22)

   b. Your prayers are answered when you GET RID OF KNOWN SIN. David said in Psalm 66:18, "If I regard iniquity in my heart, the Lord will not hear me".

   c. Your prayers are answered when you ABIDE in Christ. Live close to Jesus at all times (The vine and the branches, John 15:7).

   d. Your prayers are answered when you ASK ACCORDING to His will. The Bible reveals God's will (I John 5:14-15).

   e. Your prayers are answered when you ASK IN FAITH. Bible faith expects an answer (Mark 11:22-24 and Hebrews 11:1).

   f. Your prayers are answered when, your MOTIVES ARE RIGHT. When your motives are right and you are willing to do anything to accomplish God's will, He will give you whatever you need. (John 15:1-17 and Hebrews 4:12)

4. **JESUS TEACHES EIGHT PRACTICAL STEPS TO PRAYER IN MATTHEW 6:9-13**

   a. Address the Father DIRECTLY.
      We NOW HAVE DIRECT ACCESS TO THE FATHER.
   b. Begin with worship.
   c. Include thanksgiving.
   d. Confess your sins and ask forgiveness.
   e. Be reconciled with others.
   f. Pray for personal needs.
   g. Intercede for others.
   h. Conclude your prayer in the name of Jesus (John 16:23).

5. **PRACTICAL HELPS FOR PRAYER**

   a. Make a list. Record the answers when they come.
   b. Find a private place to pray.
   c. Have a regular time each day for prayer.
   d. Study Bible prayers and pray in accordance with scripture.
   e. As you grow in the things of God, you will find it is possible to pray without ceasing.

PRAYER - REVIEW

1. Briefly give the seven facts of what prayer is.

   a.
   b.
   c.
   d.
   e.
   f.
   g.

2. Name the five different types of prayer mentioned in our lesson.

   a.   b.   c.
   d.   e.

3. According to I John 3:22, what must we do to have our prayers answered?

4. If you are a Christian and have known sin in your life, will God answer your prayers? Quote Psalm 66:18 by memory.

5. Give the six basics of answered prayer.

   a.
   b.
   c.
   d.
   e.
   f.

6. Name the eight steps to prayer in Matthew 6:9-13.

   a.
   b.
   c.
   d.
   e.
   f.
   g.
   h.

7. From memory, quote the prayer in Matthew 6:9-13.

II PETER 1:2-11

2. Do you want more and more of God's kindness and peace? Then learn to know Him better and better.

3. For as you know Him better, He will give you, through His great power, everything you need for living a truly good life: He even shares His own glory and His own goodness with us!

4. And by that same MIGHTY POWER He has given us ALL THE OTHER RICH AND WONDERFUL BLESSINGS HE PROMISED: FOR INSTANCE, THE PROMISE TO SAVE US FROM THE LUST AND ROTTENNESS ALL AROUND US, AND TO GIVE US HIS OWN CHARACTER.

5. But to obtain these gifts, you need more than faith; you must also work hard to be good, and even that is not enough. For then you must learn to know God better and discover what He wants you to do.

6. Next, learn to put aside your own desires so that you will become patient and godly, gladly letting God have His way with you.

7. This will make possible the next step, which is for you to enjoy other people and to like them, and finally you will grow to love them deeply.

8. The more you go on in this way, the more you will grow strong spiritually and become fruitful and useful to our Lord Jesus Christ.

9. But anyone who fails to go after these additions to faith is blind indeed, or at least very shortsighted, and has forgotten that God delivered him from the old life of sin so that now he can live a strong, good life for the Lord.

10. So, dear brothers, work hard to prove that you really are among those God has called and chosen, and then you will never stumble or fall away.

11. AND GOD WILL OPEN WIDE THE GATES OF HEAVEN FOR YOU TO ENTER INTO THE ETERNAL KINGDOM OF OUR LORD AND SAVIOR JESUS CHRIST!

Scripture quotations are taken from *The Living Bible*, copyright 1971.
Used by permission of Tyndale House Publishers, Inc. Wheaton IL, 60189 USA,
All rights reserved.

APPLICATIONS OF PRAYER

Most of our prayer is under stress. When we have heavy needs, we put all of our thoughts into a prayer sack, so to speak, shake it up and throw it up toward heaven. Then we start hoping someone heard us, and just maybe something can be done about our dilemma.

At the Last Supper Jesus taught that under the NEW COVENANT, God's people HAVE BEEN GIVEN A NEW APPROACH AND DIRECT ACCESS TO GOD, WHO HAS NOW BECOME OUR HEAVENLY FATHER (Through being born again--refer to John, chapter 3). We now have DIRECT ACCESS to our Heavenly Father through Jesus Name. Hebrews 4:16 tells us to "COME BOLDLY to the THRONE of GRACE."

Jesus said in John 16:23-28, "And in that day, you shall ask me nothing, you shall ask the Father in MY NAME". Hebrews 7:12-28 refers to the better covenant. Paul refers to "Praying with all manner of prayer", in Ephesians 6:18. This strongly implies that there are different applications to prayer that we should examine.

In this lesson on prayer, we will look at three basic applications oF prayer. They are. DIRECT ACCESS TO GOD, HOW TO APPROACH THE FATHER, and PRAYING IN FAITH. To help you to be aware that there is so much more available, through prayer, additional prayer applications are listed.

1. HOW TO APPROACH THE FATHER.

2. TAKING A STANCE OF FAITH. This covers what do we do while we are waiting on God to answer our prayer.

3. THE PRAYER OF BINDING AND LOOSING. This covers breaking the enemy's power.

4. THE PRAYER OF INTERCESSION.

5. THE PRAYER OF FAITH. This is connected to the gifts described in I Corinthians 12:1-14. Review the faith given to every person in Romans 12:1-10

6. PRAYING IN TONGUES. This is connected to the, PROMISE OF THE FATHER and the utterance gifts described in I Corinthians 12:1-14 and Romans 8:26-28.

7. UNITED PRAYER and AGREEMENT IN PRAYER.

8. PETITIONAL PRAYER. For our needs to be met.

9. PRAYER of CONSECRATION and DEDICATION.

10. FELLOWSHIP WITH THE FATHER.

11. PRAISE--WORSHIP--GIVING THANKS—AND--MINISTERING UNTO THE LORD.

HOW TO APPROACH GOD

1. Decide what you need from God. Look up the scriptures relative to the need. Next meditate on them (Joshua 1:8). Remember, the 3-7 sets of scripture principal in Lesson 2.

2. Examine your life to be sure your motivations are right before God (Hebrews 4:12). If you find something in your life like sin, attitudes etc, now is the time to deal with it (I John 1:9 and James 4:3).

3. Learn to be in one accord with God, His Word, and the body of Christ. How can two walk together unless they agree? We must learn to forgive (Mark 11:25-26 and Ephesians 4:29-32). Review, The Pathway to Inner Peace lesson 10.

4. Take this time to build yourself spiritually by singing praises and praying in the spirit. Look at Jude 1:20 and I Corinthians 14:4. Snuggle up to your Father.

5. As a child of God, start talking to your Father, speaking to Him in Jesus' Name (John 16:23-24 and Hebrews 4:16). Set forth your case, and put your Father in remembrance (Philippians 4:4-7 and Isaiah 43:25-26).

6. Learn to depend on the Holy Spirit to help you in your prayer life (Romans 8:26-28). The Holy Spirit makes intercession for us as we pray.

7. Pray expecting results. BELIEVE FIRST, CONFESSION, SECOND, ANSWERS THIRD, and FEELINGS FORTH. (Mark 11:23-24 and Romans 10:9-10).

8. Thank God in advance for the answer. Praise Him and meditate on His greatness. Count your blessings, and your faith will grow.

9. Make every prayer relative to your request a statement of faith, praise, and thanksgiving. Review, TAKING A STANCE OF FAITH in this lesson on page 31.

10. NO NEGATIVE THINKING OR TALKING (Romans 12:1-2 & II Corinthians 10:3-6). We can talk ourselves out of the answers to our prayers.

WITH GOD ALL THINGS ARE POSSIBLE

TAKING A STANCE OF FAITH
AFTER WE HAVE PRAYED THE PRAYER OF FAITH

1. **We change our approach and tone of praying to an attitude of praise and thanksgiving. Casting all our care upon Him (I Peter 5:7).**

    I Peter 3:12 God hears our prayer.

    I John 5:14-15 This is the confidence we have.

    John 15:7 If you abide in ME and MY WORD abides in you. This is Rhema, the Holy Spirit's revelation to you.

    I Samuel 1:18 Example of a right attitude (before the answer comes). Hannah was told to go in peace, she ate and was not sad anymore.

2. **We set forth our case--putting our Father in remembrance (Philippians 4:4-7 and Isaiah 43:25).**

    Hebrews 4:9-16 God has a rest for us.

    Isaiah 26:3 God can keep you in perfect peace.

    I Peter 5:7 Cast all of our care upon Him.

3. **Let every thought and desire affirm you have what you ask for; do not be double minded (James 1:8).**

    Romans 12:2 Be ye transformed with the renewing of your mind.

    II Corinthians 10:3-7 Learn to control your thoughts.

    Philippians 2:5 Let this mind be in you, which was in Christ.

4. **Stay away from NEGATIVE SURROUNDINGS (Galatians 5:23-26).**

    Hebrews 3:6-14 HOLD fast to your confession.

    Hebrews 13:5-6 Jesus will NEVER leave you nor FORSAKE you.

    Ephesians 6:10-18 KEEP STANDING

    Romans 8:1-39 WE ARE MORE THAN CONQUERORS.

TAKING A STANCE OF FAITH
AFTER WE HAVE PRAYED THE PRAYER OF FAITH

5. Stay in CLOSE CONTACT WITH GOD. SNUGGLE UP to Him.

   Jeremiah 29:11-14, HE KNOWS THE PLANS HE HAS FOR YOU.

   Hebrews 11:6   God REWARDS those who DILIGENTLY SEEK HIM.

   Ephesians 3:16-21, BE STRENGTHENED THROUGH THE INNER MAN.

6. **MEDITATE CONSTANTLY on the verses you BASED YOUR PRAYER REQUEST ON (Joshua 1:8).**

   Romans 12:2   Your THOUGHT LIFE MUST BE TRANSFORMED.

   Romans 10:9-10   BELIEVE WITH YOUR HEART AND CONFESS WITH YOUR MOUTH. (THIS IS THE KEY TO RECEIVE OUR NEEDS FROM THE LORD.) Start confessing WHAT GOD'S WORD SAYS YOU ARE AND WHAT YOU HAVE IN CHRIST JESUS.

   II Timothy 2:15   STUDY to show yourself approved unto God.

7. **SEE OR ENVISION yourself with the answer to your prayers and thank your HEAVENLY FATHER for FULFILLING HIS WORD IN YOUR LIFE (Joshua 1:8). This is part of Devotion time.**

   Ephesians 1:1-23   The exceeding greatness of His POWER to us.

   Philippians 4:4-23   I can do all things through Christ Jesus.

   I Peter 1:1-9   GRACE unto you and PEACE BE MULTIPLIED.

   I Peter 5:6-10   GOD WILL, PERFECT, ESTABLISH, STRENGTHEN, AND SETTLE YOU.

God has made provision for your every need,
SPIRIT, SOUL AND BODY.

Review the Scriptural Healing lesson 8.

LESSON – 4

THE DEVOTIONAL LIFE

THE DEVOTIONAL LIFE

The differences in PRAYER and DEVOTIONS are;

Prayer is usually a time of making a *REQUEST* to the Father and DEVOTIONS is a TIME OF FELLOWSHIP WITH THE FATHER *AND / OR A TIME OF MEDITATING ON HIS WORD*. This is our opportunity to cultivate a deeper relationship with our Heavenly Father and Jesus our Lord. (SNUGGLE TIME)

This is an excellent time for SIFTING GOD'S WORD FROM THE HEAD TO THE HEART and PURIFYING THE WORD IN OUR HEART. This has been covered in the How to Study God's Word lesson.

Some of the better scriptures to use in your devotions are The Psalms, Proverbs, the Gospel of John and 1st, 2nd, & 3rd John. The In Him verses on page 14, have 140 verses telling us how we fit into the Kingdom of God. Meditating on the SEVEN COMPOUND NAMES OF GOD that are in the Scriptural Healing lesson will be very helpful also.

All of the EXTRA HELPS in the Study Manual ARE FOCUSING YOU TOWARD YOUR HEAVENLY FATHER AND YOUR POSITION IN HIM. There is enough material in this manual, along with your Bible, to assist you in your Devotional time and SPIRITUAL GROWTH for a very long time. This will HELP you to BUILD A VERY STRONG SPIRITUAL FOUNDATION IN JESUS, GOD'S SON, with Him being your CHIEF CORNER STONE.

HOW DO WE REACT TO SITUATIONS THAT COME UP IN LIFE?

We react to situations that happen to us based on comparing them to the things of our past, things in our current life and their impact on our future, our family, our friends, work, etc.

Let's compare our reaction to winning a lottery for 5 million dollars with no strings attached. We would be jumping for joy, telling everyone of our good fortune. YES!

THE DEVOTIONAL LIFE

Now let's COMPARE THIS to becoming Born-Again and having an INTIMATE, LOVING RELATIONSHIP WITH GOD WHO CREATED EVERYTHING AND HAS GIVEN US ETERNAL LIFE AND ALL THINGS THAT PERTAIN TO OUR PRESENT LIFE NOW, AND TO OUR FUTURE LIFE WITH HIM IN HEAVEN.

ARE WE REACTING IN A SIMILAR MANNER TO THIS GIFT FROM OUR HEAVENLY FATHER? I THINK NOT, AND, WHY NOT?

It is BECAUSE, OUR BABY BORN-AGAIN SPIRIT HASN'T GRASP THE REALITY TO WHAT HAS ACTUALLY TAKEN PLACE IN OUR LIFE AND REALIZED THE INDESCRIBABLE GIFT, OUR HEAVENLY FATHER HAS GIVEN US.

We have not yet, developed THE CAPACITY TO COMPARE THE THINGS OF EARTH TO THE THINGS OF HEAVEN. Jesus said, each of you (us), individually, is worth more than the entire world and all of the things there in. There is no question that the value that God and Jesus has placed on you (us) is many times more valuable, than a mere five million-dollar check.

Paul says in I Corinthians 2:14-15 "The natural man (or the unlearned Born-Again person) DOESN'T UNDERSTAND THE THINGS OF GOD, BUT THE SPIRITUAL MAN DOES". NOTICE; Paul did not say, THE SPIRITUAL BABE UNDERSTANDS.

The DEVOTION TIME will help bring our UNDERSTANDING INTO AGREEMENT WITH GOD'S PERSPECTIVE (Romans 12:1-2). Beginning as a BABE IN CHRIST, we progress in understanding, (RHEMA) as we grow toward SPIRITUAL MATURITY. Refer to THE FOUR STAGES OF SPIRITUAL GROWTH on page 13 of lesson one.

Remember: The PURPOSE of this Study is to give you the FOCUS and the Tools, to REACH A LEVEL OF RELATIONSHIP AND MATURITY IN YOUR
LORD AS QUICKLY AND SMOOTHLY AS POSSIBLE.

ALSO, This STUDY MANUAL is NOT a substitute for the Bible. It is a tool designed to assist you in your Bible studies, to help you search the Scriptures DAILY, so that you may learn for yourself, what your Lord is saying to you (Acts 17:11).

THE DEVOTIONAL LIFE
Page 3

It is the Christian's privilege to have fellowship with God every day-- communicating with Him and enjoying His presence.

This fellowship is a two-way matter. God speaks to us through the Scriptures and the Holy Spirit, and we speak to Him by prayer. This two-way fellowship with the Lord is a daily necessity if our goal is to know and please Him.

The Bible is our handbook for daily fellowship with God, the means by which He speaks to us in a living, practical way as the Holy Spirit gives us understanding.

LEARNING FROM DAVID'S DEVOTION

God called David, "a man after my own heart" (Acts 13:22). David wrote many of the Psalms, and they show the depth and richness of his relationship with God.

Look up the following verses in the Psalms and record what each one tells you about David's relationship with God. As you write the answer, think about how you can respond to God the same way.

5:3

25:5

32:5

34:4

51:10

55:17

62:1

63:1

103:1-2

145:1

THE DEVOTIONAL LIFE

THE EXAMPLE OF JESUS

1. What evidence do you see in Luke 5:15-16 that Jesus considered time alone with His Father to be very important?

2. What did Jesus do just before choosing His twelve apostles (Luke 6:12-13)?

3. Read Luke 22:39-44 which describes a portion of the night before Jesus died. How did Jesus show His continued closeness to God?

4. In Luke 23:46 what were Jesus' last words before He died?

5. What has God called us to according to I Corinthians 1:9?

6. Read Ephesians 3:12. Because of our faith in Christ, what attitude can we have in approaching God?

7. Review your answers in this chapter. On the basis of what you learned, summarize here how important you believe it is for you to maintain a close relationship with God, and explain why you feel that way.

8. Men and women of God through the ages have made it a habit to spend time privately with Him each day, generally early in the morning. Complete the following statements to help you plan time with God every day. Start small with an amount of time you can easily maintain. Plan to let this daily fellowship with God be a regular and increasing part of your schedule.

MY DAILY APPOINTMENT WITH GOD

MY BEST TIME EACH DAY IS_____.

I PLAN TO ALLOW APPROXIMATELY_____ MINUTES FOR MY LORD.

MY BEST PLACE FOR MEETING GOD ALONE IN FELLOWSHIP IS_____.

What Is GOD'S Snuggle Package?

IT IS!

THE NIGHT OF THE LAST SUPPER

JESUS' FINAL INSTRUCTIONS TO US.

THE PROMISE OF THE FATHER

YOU SHALL RECEIVE POWER

JOHN 7:37-39

THE RIVERS OF LIVING WATER IS THE BAPTISM IN ACTION

REVELATION 3:20

I AM KNOCKING AT YOUR DOOR

MATTHEW 6:33

SEEK YE FIRST

LUKE 11:13

HOW MUCH MORE

GALATIANS 5:13-26

THE FRUIT IS GOD'S CHARACTER

II PETER 1:2-11

GET TO KNOW GOD BETTER

COLOSSIANS 1:9-27 AND 3:8-17

PUT OFF THE OLD MAN

PRAISE AND WORSHIP - PSALMS 148-150

GIVING THANKS TO THE LORD AND GROWING IN OUR CAPACITY TO PRAISE HIM.

NOTES

LESSON - 5

THE PROMISE OF THE FATHER

THE THREE PRIORITIES OF GOD

We want to discuss the Promise of The Father and why the Father is saying..."Tarry in Jerusalem (Where you live) until endued with Power From on High".

We need to look at God's three priorities first which are..

1. God is looking for People that will WORSHIP HIM IN SPIRIT AND TRUTH. John Ch. 4:24
2. God sent His Son that we might receive eternal life. Jesus died on the cross John Ch. 3:1-21.
3. God sent His Holy Spirit to EMPOWER us, "Wait for the Promise." Acts 1:8

We want to look at THE REASON why the Promise is one of God's priorities. There has been continuous opposition and spiritual warfare starting with Adam and Eve. Satan has always tried to cause people to question God's Word and distorting the truth. Satan has been stealing from and destroying God's people from day one.

When Satan thought he was going to be uprooted at Moses' time he had all the babies killed starting at 2 years old and under. When he thought that a new king was going to uproot him around the time of the birth of Jesus he had all the babies killed from 2 years old and under.

Israel has been under attack every since God designated her, as His chosen People. Remember, the Old Testament History, concerning Israel, and what is happening in our time, World War One and Two, May 14, 1948 and the 1967 war etc. Israel is still under attack today.

As we move to the New Testament, we see that the Bride, of the Son of God, has been under continuous attack from day one. The Jewish leaders were continually attacking the church. We don't have room to cover the persecution of the Christian believers by the Roman Empire. Saul before he was converted was having people arrested, put in prison and even killed for their faith. Saul was guilty of murder.

Years later after being converted Paul wrote in Ephesians Ch.6, "We are not fighting flesh and blood but powers and principalities of powers in heavenly places". Paul basically was saying there is a military type structure in Satan's kingdom and if we could see what was happening in the spiritual world with our natural eyes we would drop in a faint. If we could see the satanic activity, it would appear like the big hurricane that swept through the Bahamas and the east coast in Sept. 1999. REMEMBER; the enemy has a minimum of **6000** years of experience. **Most Christians are unaware that they even have an enemy.**

The bible says, that in the last days the enemy will come in like a flood, **but God will raise up a standard.** I believe that standard is the Bride of God's Son, filled with the Holy Spirit, being obedient to what the Father has asked her to do.

Let's look at some of the strategies Satan has used against the church.

Most people are taught, **not to talk politics or religion.** **But the Bible says**, to go into **ALL** of the world and tell every PERSON, beginning in your own hometown.

People are taught that Christian's are meek, weak and well reserved. **The Bible say's**, that we are more than conquerors.

Satan has confused the church on many theological issues. **The Bible says we should come to the unity of faith.** Some of the older denominations, have had a problem in saying what the Bible says, such as, preaching and teaching, you must be Born-Again. They use terms like, "I've made my peace with God".

There is confusion in regard to water baptism. Some sprinkle and some dunk. Others teach you are not saved unless you have been baptized in water.

There is major confusion on whether or not we can lose our salvation.

There is major confusion on whether the gifts of the spirit are still active today or not.

Probably, the most arguments are over, the Promise of the Father, known also as being filled with the Holy Spirit and or being baptized in the Holy Spirit.

We are in the last days and that means Satan has pulled out all stops to stop God's plan and to destroy and contaminate the Bride of God's Son. His main attack is to distort God's Word, and create confusion and division in the church. We are seeing 6000 years of prophecy being fulfilled in our day.

We are in the midst of a very major spiritual warfare and **our Father says**; "If you fight the battle my way, you can stand still and see the salvation of the Lord". We need every resource our Lord has given us. Jesus said, "You shall receive POWER after the Holy Spirit has come up on you." Acts 1:8

Paul said in I Corinthians 10:3-6; "Our weapons of warfare are not natural----weapons ---but they are spiritual for breaking down the strongholds of imagination and everything else that would exalt itself against God."
Jesus said; "Cheer up, I have overcome the world, Peace I leave you, Peace I give you. My yoke is easy and my burden is light".
John 14:27-28, John 16:31-33 and Matthew 11:25-30

How can we experience, *this peace and power*, Jesus talked about the night of the Last Supper and be more than conquerors?

OUR ANSWER IS!

Through the Promise of the Father and coming to Jesus WHO IS the author and finisher of our faith and letting Him baptize us in the Holy Spirit. Hebrews 12:1-2, Matthew 3:11 and Acts 10:34-48

Jesus is THE ONE WHO baptizes us in the Holy Spirit. We will be opening ourselves to receive what Jesus had while He was here on earth. (Acts 10:38) Any minister can baptize us in water in obedience to the Lord's instructions, but only Jesus can baptize us in the Holy Spirit.

Receiving the Promise of the Father is SIMILAR TO receiving Jesus as your personal savior.

- We don't deserve it. And...
- We can't buy it.
- Our goodness and righteousness doesn't qualify us for the promise.

It is given, because the Father loves us that much, and His grace is that wonderful!

To be all that your Father wants you to be, is connected to the Promise of the Father. The Promise will give us (you) the spiritual back-bone we need to live the life that is pleasing to the Lord. Look at Peter before and after the day of Pentecost.

In John Ch. 17:15 Jesus asks the Father not to take us out of the world, but that the Father would keep us from the evil of the world. Jesus also said in Acts 1:1-8, "you shall receive power *AFTER,* the Holy Spirit comes upon you."

REVIEW; II Peter 2:2-11 on page 28.

SO, HOW DO WE RECEIVE THIS BLESSING?

WHILE WE ARE PRAISING AND WORSHIPPING OUR LORD, WE ASK HIM, TO FILL US TO OVER FLOWING, WITH THE HOLY SPIRIT ACCORDING TO THE BOOK OF ACTS. AMEN

THE PROMISE OF THE FATHER
VERSUS THE GIFTS OF THE SPIRIT

IN THE OLD TESTAMENT God said, I will be their God; I will live with them. They will be my children, and I WILL BE IN THEM.

IN THE NEW TESTAMENT

Jesus talked about the gift or the promise of the Father. In John 4 Jesus said God is a Spirit, and He is looking for people to WORSHIP HIM IN SPIRIT AND IN TRUTH.

In John chapters 13-17, the night of THE LAST SUPPER, Jesus FOCUSED ON THE HOLY SPIRIT. Jesus had SAVED THE BEST FOR THE LAST.

Acts 1:4-8: Jesus said, "TARRY IN JERUSALEM, AND WAIT FOR THE PROMISE OF THE FATHER." (DON'T LEAVE TOWN WITHOUT IT) The Promise of The Father is, the Baptism of the Holy Spirit. The Baptism of the Holy Spirit is for the individual to cultivate a DEEPER RELATIONSHIP with God, who is a Spirit, and for an increased Spiritual Power level. The Baptism includes the personal, private language of tongues to develop a two-way communication with our Heavenly Father.

IN ADDITION TO ALL OF THIS

Jesus gave gifts: Matthew 3:11, Acts 2:1-4 and Ephesians 4:7-16
The Holy Spirit gives gifts: I Corinthians 12:1-11, 28-30.

The **IMPORTANT POINT** IS, the GIFT of TONGUES given with the BAPTISM of (in) THE HOLY SPIRIT, is a DIFFERENT GIFT from the TONGUES given in I Corinthians chapter 12.

There **is a DIFFERENCE** between the "Promise of the Father" in contrast to the Gifts of the Holy Spirit. This represents **two** different givers and **two** different gifts. One gift is for a personal fellowship with the Father, and the other is for the benefit of the Church and other applications of ministry and for God to speak directly to the body. That is why Paul says, **"DIVERSITY** OF TONGUES."

If we use I Corinthians 13:8 to throw out tongues then we become UNLEARNED because prophecies and knowledge are included in that verse also. Look at I Corinthians 14:16, 23 and Mark 16:14-20.

But rather, Paul says, "Praying in tongues builds you up spiritually"
 I Corinthians 14:4.

I Corinthians chapter 14 REGULATES the Gifts of The Spirit in chapter 12. It does not REGULATE your personal relationship and communication in tongues with your Heavenly Father that is included with the Promise.

THE PROMISE OF THE FATHER
THE BAPTISM WITH THE HOLY SPIRIT

INTRODUCTION
The Holy Spirit is the third person of the Godhead. He is not an "it" or a "thing."
HE IS GOD, THE HOLY SPIRIT.

Refer to THE HOLY SPIRIT - A CLOSER LOOK on page 48.

THE HOLY SPIRIT HAS:

    a. **A Mind:**   He searcheth the hearts and knows the mind of the spirit (the inner man). Romans 8:27 and Hebrews 4:12
    b. **A Will:**   He divideth spiritual gifts as He wills I Corinthians 12:11.
    c. **Feelings:**   We as believers are exhorted, DO NOT GRIEVE THE HOLY SPIRIT OF GOD. Ephesians 4:30
    Also, do not quench or resist the Holy Spirit.

THE HOLY SPIRIT CAN:

    a. **Speak:**   He that hath an ear let him hear what the Spirit SAITH to the churches Revelation 2:7.
    b. **Teach:**   He shall TEACH you all things, John 14:26.
    c. **Guide:**   He will GUIDE you into all truth, John 16:13.
    d. **Comfort:**   He will ABIDE with you forever, John 14:16.
    e. **Call:**   HE CALLED and sent forth Barnabas and Paul into the ministry, Acts 13:2.

1. THE PROMISED BAPTISM

John the Baptist was noted for baptizing people in water unto repentance. He said that Jesus would baptize with the Holy Spirit, John 1:32-33.

The woman at the well was told about "the living water." They that worship God must worship Him in spirit and in truth, John 4:1-24.

It is the Spirit that quickeneth (Gives life) John 6:63.

Out of your belly shall flow rivers of living water. This was prophecy concerning the "Promise of the Father." John 7:37-39.

Ye know Him, for He dwelleth WITH YOU AND SHALL BE IN YOU.
John 14:16-17.

I have many more things to say unto you but, you cannot bare them now (understand). When the Holy Spirit comes, He will remind you of everything I have said and He will be your TEACHER.
John 16:7-15

THE PROMISE OF THE FATHER
THE BAPTISM WITH THE HOLY SPIRIT
Page 2

Jesus instructs the believers: Wait for the PROMISE OF THE FATHER. YE SHALL RECEIVE POWER AFTER THE HOLY SPIRIT HAS COME UPON YOU. Acts 1:1-8

Peter preached about the PROMISE of the Father under the power of the Holy Spirit. He was quoting, Joel 2:28-29 in Acts 2:1-36.

2. **THE PROMISE FULFILLED**

Luke 4:1	Jesus and Acts 10:38
Acts 2:4	The 120 in the upper room
Acts 4:8	Peter
Acts 4:31	Peter, James, and John
Acts 7:55	Stephen
Acts 8:14	The Samaritans (about two years later)
Acts 10:44-46	Cornelius and household (6 years later)
Acts 11:24	Barnabus
Acts 13:9	Paul
Acts 13:52	Disciples
Acts 19:1-6	Ephesians (about 20 years later)

3. **TWO IMPORTANT ELEMENTS IN RECEIVING THE BAPTISM ARE, BEING BORN AGAIN AND BEING SPIRITUALLY THIRSTY.**

Luke 5:37-38   Parable of the new wine in old bottles.

   NOTE: WHAT IS A PARABLE? A parable is an earthly truth with a Heavenly meaning.

John 7:37-39   If any man (you) thirst, out of his (your) belly shall flow rivers of living water.

John 4:14   The water I shall give him (you) shall be in him (you) a well of water springing up unto everlasting life.

Revelation 22:17 Let him (you) that is thirsty **come, take of the water of life freely.**
Look also at Revelation 3:20

Isaiah 12:3 . . . . . **YOU CAN**, draw out of the well of salvation WITH JOY.

THE PROMISE OF THE FATHER
THE BAPTISM WITH THE HOLY SPIRIT
Page 3

4. **WHAT MUST I DO TO RECEIVE THE BAPTISM WITH THE HOLY SPIRIT?**

   Hebrews 12:1-2   LOOK to Jesus, the AUTHOR and FINISHER of your faith. Jesus is the Baptizer.

   Luke 24:49   Behold, I send the PROMISE of my Father upon you, BUT TARRY ye in Jerusalem until ye be endued with POWER from on high. DON'T GIVE UP. THIS PROMISE IS YOURS.

   Acts 2:38-39   This promise is for as many as the Lord calls. The word, *"WHOSOEVER"* means *YOU TOO!*

   John 7:37-38   Jesus said, "If any man (you) THIRST, let him (you) COME UNTO ME, AND DRINK. He (you) that BELIEVETH on Me, as the SCRIPTURE HAS SAID, OUT OF his (your) belly shall FLOW RIVERS OF LIVING WATER."

   Luke 11:11-13   ASK and it SHALL BE GIVEN YOU.

   Acts 2:4   The scriptural evidence is that you will find yourself praising God in your NEW PRAYER LANGUAGE, which you did not have before (tongues).

   NOTE: YOUR HEAVENLY FATHER AND YOUR LORD AND SAVIOR JESUS CHRIST WANT YOU TO RELAX AND LET THEM BESTOW THEIR DIVINE LOVE GIFT UPON YOU.

   Psalm 22:3   The Lord inhabits the praises of His people.

   Psalm 148-150   PRAISE YE THE LORD FOR HE IS WORTHY!

5. **TWO OF THE BEST ENVIRONMENTS TO RECEIVE THE BAPTISM**

   a. When there is a worship time around the altar and spirit-filled people are there to pray with you.

   b. When you are having private devotions at home and you are focusing in on the Lord with all your heart.

   The Lord is not concerned about where you are as much as He is concerned about where your heart and mind are like your attitude toward Him AND HIS WORD.

THE PROMISE OF THE FATHER:
THE BAPTISM WITH THE HOLY SPIRIT
- REVIEW -

1. Who is the Holy Spirit?

2. What three elements does the Holy Spirit have?
   a.
   b.
   c.

3. In the lesson there are five attributes mentioned concerning the Holy Spirit. What are they? Give scripture also.
   a.
   b.
   c.
   d.
   e.

4. According to Acts 1:1-8, what were the last words of Jesus before He was taken up to heaven?

5. According to John 16:12-13, why was the Holy Spirit given to the believers?

6. Name two important elements in receiving the Baptism of the Holy Spirit.
   a.
   b.

7. What is a parable?

8. What must you do to receive the Holy Spirit?
   a.
   b.
   c.

9. What will defeat the purpose of the "Love Gifts?"

10. Why do Christians need this experience in their lives?

11. Have you received the Baptism of the Holy Spirit with the biblical evidence of speaking in a heavenly language?

THE BAPTISM WITH THE HOLY SPIRIT
- OBSERVATIONS -

1. In every scriptural case, ALL who were open and seeking were filled.

2. After the day of PENTECOST every individual that received the baptism with the Holy Spirit was a NEW CONVERT, except those at Ephesus. They had not heard there was a Holy Spirit yet. They did receive after they were taught.

3. The fullness of the Spirit was ALWAYS RECEIVED BY FAITH after or at the same time the WORD was ministered.

4. In each case there was an outward evidence of praise in an UNLEARNED HEAVEN-SENT LANGUAGE.

5. The INDWELLING SPIRIT brings ETERNAL LIFE, but the FULLNESS (baptism) of the SPIRIT BRINGS POWER for living a sinless life and the necessary POWER to serve God in the way He wants you to.

6. Something always happens "WITHIN" when we come to God in FAITH, trusting Him to be TRUE TO HIS WORD.

7. When asking for the INFILLING of the Spirit, we need not fear. We are coming at God's invitation (Ephesians 5:18).

8. NONE of the gifts of God's Son, nor His Spirit, are a mark of our maturity. They are an EXPRESSION OF HIS GRACE whereby we can progressively fulfill His perfect will in our lives (Ephesians 4:1-16).

9. The spiritual gifts are not a sign of holiness. They are a sign that THE SANCTIFIER has come, and HIS WORK WILL PROCEED as the WORD IS OBEYED.

10. Nothing DEFEATS the purpose of any LOVE GIFT, other than for the recipient of it, to put the gift before the giver.

11. A LIFE of FELLOWSHIP with the GIVER should be THE DESIRE and GOAL of all those who seek the baptism with the Holy Spirit.

12. The baptism with the Holy Spirit produces the ABIDING CHARACTER of God, which changes a person's WALK AND TALK.

LET JESUS BAPTIZE YOU NOW.

THE HOLY SPIRIT - A CLOSER LOOK

The Holy Spirit is God and is equal to the Father and the Son. Don't ever refer to Him as an "it" or refer to Him as an influence.

He is God, The Holy Spirit, and is set forth in the Bible as being distinct from the Father and the Son. In the Genesis account of creation, He is seen actively engaged in the work of creation along with the Father and the Son.

In the Old Testament HE CAME UPON MEN TO EMPOWER THEM FOR SERVICE, but when they were disobedient He departed from them. When David sinned against the Lord he prayed, "Take not thy Holy Spirit from me."

In the New Testament, AFTER PENTECOST, we see the Holy Spirit indwelling in the believer, never to leave him, filling, and empowering him for service.

The study of the PERSON AND THE WORK OF THE HOLY SPIRIT IS OF THE UTMOST IMPORTANCE. A scriptural understanding of God The Holy Spirit will make you a STRONGER Christian and servant of God. THE HOLY SPIRIT IS IN YOUR BODY.

a. THE DEITY OF THE HOLY SPIRIT
   Hebrews. 9:14; Luke 1:35; Genesis 1:2

b. THE EMBLEMS OF THE HOLY SPIRIT
   Luke 3:16 - Also, The Dove, Water, and Oil, etc.

c. THE SINS AGAINST THE HOLY SPIRIT
   Matthew 12:31-32 - Also, DO NOT QUENCH, GRIEVE, OR RESIST THE HOLY SPIRIT.

d. THE WORK OF THE HOLY SPIRIT
   John 16:7-14

e. THE FRUIT OF THE HOLY SPIRIT
   Galatians 5:22-23

f. MORE SCRIPTURE:

Matthew 28:19	Acts 1:4-8
I John 5:7	Acts 2:4
Hebrews 9:14	Acts 8:17-19
Luke 24:49	Acts 9:17-18
I Corinthians 13:4-10	Acts 10:44-46
John 14:17	Acts 11:15-16
Romans 8:9	Acts 19:16
I Corinthians 6:19	Acts 15:8-9
II Timothy 1:14	Revelation 3:20
I John 2:27 & 3:24	Colossians 1:27

NOTE; Used by permission of Thomas Nelson, Inc.

LESSON -6

THE LEADERSHIP OF THE HOLY SPIRIT

NOTES - THE LEADERSHIP OF THE HOLY SPIRIT

During THE NIGHT OF THE LAST SUPPER, John chapters 13-17 and pages 3-7 in this book, Jesus opened the DOOR FOR A SPIRIT TO SPIRIT RELATIONSHIP with the Father and Son through the PERSON OF THE HOLY SPIRT.

By being born-again we have direct access to our Heavenly Father and our Lord who gave His life for us.

Now we want to examine the TWO-WAY COMMUNICATION with our Heavenly Father and Lord that is included when we receive the PROMISE of the Father. The PURPOSE of this lesson is to introduce you to this COMUNICATION PROVISION your Father has given you.

If you have the confidence the Holy Spirit is in you and your Heavenly Father wants to speak to you, through the person of the Holy Spirit, then your faith will allow the Holy Spirit to talk to you and do all the other exciting things the Lord wants to do in your life. This communication growth is a MAJOR FAITH BUILDER because, once you are confident your Father has said something to you, you will be able to believe Him and be able to respond to Him in child-like faith, confidence and most importantly, obedience.

OUR TWO GREATEST TASKS ARE;

1. As an ADULT, being able to DEVELOP CHILD LIKE FAITH in our Heavenly Father.

2. Learning to CONSISTANTLY HEAR, our Father talk to us.

LEADERSHIP OF THE HOLY SPIRIT

1. **REVIEW THE NIGHT OF THE LAST SUPPER**

    a. It was the Father and Son's plan to send the person of the Holy Spirit to live with you and be in you. (I Corinthians 3:16--YOU ARE THE TEMPLE OF GOD)
    b. Jesus said. "it is expedient for you that I go away so I can send the Holy Spirit". (John 16:7-15)

2. **WHAT IS THE HOLY SPIRIT SUPPOSED TO DO SINCE HE HAS COME?**

    a. To **CONVICT** of sin (John 16:5-15)
    b. To **GUIDE**
    c. To **LEAD** (Romans 8:14, Galatians 5:18)
    d. To **TEACH**
    e. To **GIVE GIFTS OF SERVICE** as in I Corinthians 12
    f. To **CALL** us to different areas of ministry

3. **PAUL SAID, THE HOLY SPIRIT IS A SURETY (A DOWN) PAYMENT TO ALL THE PROMISES THE FATHER HAS GIVEN HIS SON'S BRIDE (Ephesians 1:13-14)**

    - All of the gifts, all of the fruit, and everything else that God gives us, are THROUGH THE PERSON OF THE HOLY SPIRIT.

4. **THE HOLY SPIRIT USES MANY SOURCES TO LEAD US. HE USES:**

    a. Apostles
    b. Prophets
    c. Evangelists
    d. Pastors
    e. Teachers (Ephesians 4:1-16, I Corinthians 12:1-11)
    f. THE WRITTEN WORD - Study to show (II Timothy 2:15)
    g. Be ye transformed (Romans 12:1-2)

5. **AS WE GROW, THE HOLY SPIRIT LEADS US THROUGH OUR INNER BORN-AGAIN SPIRIT (Ephesians 1:17-23 and Ephesians 3:16-21)**

    a. The children of God are led by the Spirit of God (Romans 8:14).
    b. Through a small still voice (I Kings 19:11-13).
    c. He talks to us through our own thought process system.
    d. If you can hear yourself think, you can be trained to listen to the Holy Spirit (THE BOOK OF ACTS).
    e. The Holy Spirit speaks to our conscience.
    f. On rare occasions a vision may be given.
    g. Or, on rare occasions, a visitation of an angel or an appearance of Jesus may occur.

LEADERSHIP OF THE HOLY SPIRIT
Page 2

6. **WE ARE STRONGLY INSTRUCTED TO TEST ALL THINGS**
   There are so many voices trying to get our attention. *WHAT THREE VOICES ARE WE ABLE TO HEAR, WITH OUR INNER EAR?*

   a. Our Shepherd (John 10:7-18 and I John 4:1-3). We want to know the voice of our Shepherd (John 10:1-18).

   b. Satan, as a roaring Lion (I Peter 5:8 and Ephesians 6:10-18). We are not fighting flesh and blood but powers and principalities of powers.

   c. Ourselves, with freedom to choose right from wrong (II Corinthians 10:3-10). We want to learn to recognize the voice of our Shepherd.

   NOTE: The Holy Spirit talks to us, through our inner spirit as the small still voice. We can learn to recognize this as our Shepherd's voice.

7. **REVIEW; THE FOUR STAGES OF GROWTH.**

   a. The fourth step should be everyone's GOAL. Growing to Christian maturity is God's will for us.

   b. We should use all of God's resources to become mature in Christ.

   c. Be ready to grow in grace until Jesus comes (II Peter 3:18).

   d. We can approach our test and training the way Jesus did, or we can approach our test and training the way Israel did.

   - Jesus completed His test in forty days.

   - Israel failed after forty years.

   e. Hebrews chapter 11 says, we can be VICTORIOUS NO MATTER WHAT THE ENEMY THROWS AT US.

   f. THE KINGDOM OF GOD IS RIGHTEOUSNESS, PEACE, AND JOY IN THE HOLY SPIRIT (Romans 14:17).

   g. **GREATER IS HE THAT IS IN US THAN HE THAT IS IN THE WORLD** I John 4:4.

LET'S FINE TUNE - TRAINING OUR SPIRIT
TO BE ABLE TO LISTEN TO THE HOLY SPIRIT

1. Find a quiet place.

    - Jesus got up early to pray, Mark 1:35.

    - Habakkuk had a quiet place to pray, Habakkuk 2:1-3.

2. Start worshipping the Lord and visualize Him being right there with you. When you are born-again, He has come to live in your heart. (The Inner Man)

3. Get quiet and listen to the SPONTANEOUS THOUGHT FLOW FROM YOUR HEART. REMEMBER, THE HOLY SPIRIT DOES NOT WORK OUT OF YOUR HEAD.

4. Learn to LISTEN for the SMALL STILL VOICE that is FLOWING in our HEART.

    - We can easily break the thought flow by jumping in with our head-- similar to the way we interrupt people who are talking to us.

    - If you are feeling fractured, stressed, or rushed, the enemy has slipped in, or you could be working out of your head and not your heart.

    - If you are feeling peace, healing, and the presence of the Lord, then you are listening to the Holy Spirit.

5. Write down the SPONTANEOUS thoughts that come from your heart.

6. Test all things. After we have completed our listening and journaling, then we can compare what we have written to what the scripture says.

    - **REMEMBER: ALL THINGS ARE TO BE TESTED WITH THE WRITTEN WORD.**

7. **REVIEW;** all of the scripture used in this lesson to help you to develop the confidence that your Heavenly Father wants to speak directly to you and that He uses the person of the Holy Spirit to accomplish this.

    - **This should be a progressive exercise for the rest of our life because we are actually developing a two-way communication and fellowship with our Heavenly Father, Habakkuk 2:1-3.**

NOTES

LESSON - 7

THE
GIFTS
OF THE
HOLY SPIRIT

THE BIBLE IS THE HOLY SPIRITS TOOL BOX

I Corinthians 12:1-14 is a partial list of gifts the Holy Spirit works with. Notice how much the word "diversities of" is used. In I Corinthians 12:4-6, you see the Father, Son and Holy Spirit are working together to build up the Bride and to bring her into the unity of faith.

God – Has Given:

His only begotten Son – John 3:1-21

His Promise of the Holy Spirit – Acts 1:8

Faith – Unto every person a measure – Romans 12:3

Power – To become children of God- John 1:2

JESUS – HAS GIVEN:

HIS LIFE – For us on the cross- John 19:1-42

He is still interceding for us in Heaven- Hebrews 7:25

He gives us grace – Ephesians 4:7, 2:8-9
Please read Ephesians 4:1-32

Jesus Baptizes in the Holy Spirit – Matthew 3:11

THE HOLY SPIRIT GIVES – LEADERSHIP and GIFTS

Refer to the Night of the Last Supper

I Corinthians 12:1-13 – The Gifts

I Corinthians chapter 14, is the regulatory chapter for these gifts.

THE GIFTS OF THE HOLY SPIRIT

INTRODUCTION

There is a difference between, THE PROMISE OF THE FATHER in Acts 1:4-8 and 2:38-39 and THE GIFTS OF THE SPIRIT, in I Corinthians chapter 12. Every born-again Christian is instructed, by Jesus Himself, to pursue and receive the Promise. The PROMISE PACKAGE, includes the heavenly language of tongues to develop your personal relationship with your Heavenly Father and to give you the strength you need to live an overcoming Christian life.

The GIFTS OF THE SPIRIT in I Corinthians 12:8-11 are to DEVELOP the BODY of CHRIST to a BALANCED BODY MINISTRY and a TEAM to spread the gospel.

THE CLASSIFICATION OF GIFTS

The Gifts Of Revelation Or Instruction

The Word of Wisdom	For divine guidance	I Corinthians 12:8
The Word of Knowledge	For revealing hidden facts	I Corinthians 12:8
Discerning of Spirits	For exposing an evil spirit	I Corinthians 12:10

The Gifts Of Power Or Gifts Of Importation

The Gift of Faith	Faith beyond human ability	I Corinthians 12:9
The Gift of Healing	Physical needs, etc.	I Corinthians 12:9
The Gift of Miracles	Acts beyond the law of nature	I Corinthians 12:10

The Gifts Of Inspiration Or Gifts Of Utterance

The Gift of Prophecy	For edifying the Church	I Corinthians 12:10
The Gift of Tongues	A message to the church	I Corinthians 12:10
The Gift of Interpretation of Tongues		I Corinthians 12:10

THE GIFTS OF THE HOLY SPIRIT in *I CORINTHIANS 12:1-11.*

To each believer there is given a spiritual ennoblement and capacity for specific service. No believer is destitute of such a gift according to verses 7 and 11, but in their distribution the Holy Spirit acts in free sovereignty.

1. THE WORD OF WISDOM

This gift comes by revelation and is used in preaching and teaching the gospel of Christ, as well as being manifested in counseling and administration.

Problems will occur, delicate situations will arise, and God's revealed wisdom is needed.

When a word of wisdom is spoken, a person is deeply conscious that the supremely right thing has been said and the true course of action indicated. (I Corinthians 2:1-4, 7, 9-11).

THE GIFTS OF THE HOLY SPIRIT

2. THE WORD OF KNOWLEDGE

God has all knowledge; therefore, a revelation springing from that all-embracing knowledge can justly be described as a word of knowledge.

It is reasonable to believe that the Holy Spirit can impart a manifestation of any part of divine knowledge at any time, as He wills. The Lord reveals matters to His servants and in this way induces them with a supernatural knowledge of facts that prove most helpful.

Scriptural examples:

John 4:16-19	Jesus and the Samaritan woman.
Acts 11:28	Agabus foretells world famine.
Acts 21:11	Agabus warns Paul.

3. DISCERNING OF SPIRITS

This is a gift of spiritual insight into the spirit realm given by the Holy Spirit to the believer.

This gift reveals the true source of any supernatural manifestation.

This gift has to do with discerning of "spirits," not of men in their natural course of action (I Corinthians 2:14).

God did not leave His children defenseless. He gave us the gift of discerning of spirits (I John 4:1-3).

We are to judge the spirits that are in operation to be sure if they are of God. What they say will always line up with God's Word if they are of Him.

Our warfare is against principalities, powers, and rulers of darkness of this world, against spiritual wickedness in the "spirit realm". Refer to Ephesians 6

4. THE GIFT OF FAITH

This faith is a particular manifestation of the Holy Spirit, which is granted only to certain individuals for a certain crisis or a certain opportunity.

This gift is DIFFERENT than faith one receives to be saved (saving faith, Ephesians 2:8). No man can come to Jesus except the Father draws him (John 6:44).

Scriptural examples: Elijah challenges the prophets of Baal, I Kings 18:24-39 and Peter at the Gate Beautiful Acts 3:1-6, 16.

THE GIFTS OF THE HOLY SPIRIT

5. THE GIFT OF HEALING

It is the energy of God at work in and through the believer that brings the healing.

No reference is made to magnetic, psychic, or mental powers being at work; the glory is given directly to God.

This gift appears to be a spiritual gift especially connected with the ministry of an evangelist and often gave the apostles an open door in their evangelistic work.

Its exercise attracts the attention of people to the gospel of Christ.

Some believers seem to have faith for the healing of certain illnesses. This may be why the word "gifts" (Diversities) is used (Mark 16:17-18).

6. WORKING OF MIRACLES

The thought here is the great power of God operating by the Spirit at a given time for a particular need.

Scriptural examples:

John 2:1-11	Jesus at the marriage in Cana turns water into wine.
Acts 8:5-8	Phillip at Samaria casts out unclean spirits and healed the sick.
Acts 9:40	Peter raises Tabitha from the dead.

7. THE GIFT OF PROPHECY

This is an inspired utterance speaking from an immediate revelation as it relates to future events or as it relates to the mind of the Spirit at a given moment.

In the New Testament it appears that the gift of prophecy operated in a man and enabled him to speak "to edification and exhortation and comfort"
(I Thessalonians 2:11-13 and Acts 21:8-14).

It can sweep the church assembly up into heights of glory and enthusiasm; it can melt with tenderness and can make the church tremble with awe.

It truly ministers to the believer, and in the unbeliever it can produce deep conviction.

In its fullest purity, the gift demands a very high order of fellowship between the believer and his God.

THE GIFTS OF THE HOLY SPIRIT

8. THE GIFT OF TONGUES

The gift of tongues consists of a power of more or less ecstatic speech in languages with which the speaker is not naturally familiar.

It is a logical outcome from an intense fullness of emotion to the spirit "within." This deep spiritual emotion is manifested through prayer and the moving of the Holy Spirit (I Corinthians 14:2, 14:12-19 and Romans 8:26-39).

The revealed purpose of the gift of tongues is God's resource to speak directly to the church, to warn, to uplift, to encourage, and for any other communication He would like to impart for the building up of the body.

NOTE;
Building up your faith praying in the Holy Ghost, (tongues) is connected to THE PROMISE OF THE FATHER for your personal edification and fellowship with the Father (Jude 1:20 and I Corinthians 14:4). It is through this fellowship with the Father that He can give a message and interpretation in tongues and or a word of prophecy to the body.

9. THE GIFT OF INTERPRETATION OF TONGUES

All those who speak publicly in tongues are directed to pray for the gift of interpretation (I Corinthians 14:13).

These two gifts working together in the congregation build up and edify the church and are equal with the gift of prophecy.

NOTE: The interpretation of tongues is received through a close concentration to the leading of the HOLY SPIRIT, not by hearing the message given in tongues.

The words are given by revelation and follow the rules of all inspired utterance, coming either by vision, by burden, or by suggestion, just as the Spirit may choose.

OTHER GIFTS OF MINISTRY

Apostles, prophets, teachers, miracles, gifts of healing, helps, governments, diversities of tongues, interpretation of tongues.
I Corinthians 12:28-30

God sets these gifts in the church for the perfecting of the saints.
Ephesians 4:11-13

He gave some apostles, some prophets, some evangelists, some pastors and some teachers. In this scripture it is indicated that certain Spirit-induced men were "gifts" to the church.

THE GIFTS OF THE HOLY SPIRIT

THE CONDITIONS UNDER WHICH THE GIFTS ARE MOST LIKELY TO OPERATE

Where the **GIVER** of the gifts is not **QUENCHED**.	I Thes. 5:19
Where the **GIVER** of the gifts is not **GRIEVED**.	Ephesians 4:30
Where the **GIVER** of the gifts is not **RESISTED**.	Hebrews 3:7-19
Where the **CHURCH** is always **FILLED** with the Spirit.	Ephesians 5:18-19
Where the **Holy Spirit** is **ALLOWED** to **LEAD**.	Acts 13:2
When the **WORD OF FAITH is BEING PREACHED**.	Acts 14:9-10

Where there is a **NEED**. For example, an evil spirit is discerned by the gift of discerning of spirits and is cast out by the **POWER AND AUTHORITY** given us over evil spirits in the **NAME OF JESUS**, Acts 16:16-18. In Mark 6:7-13, the **DISCIPLES WERE SENT TWO-BY-TWO**. Review Lesson 12, for the Authority of the Believer.

> **A SPECIAL NOTE:** Look at Romans 10:8-14 and compare it to what Jesus said in Mark 11:22-26 -- believe with the heart and confess with the mouth.

THE ATTITUDE A BELIEVER SHOULD HAVE TO RECEIVE GIFTS.
(Hebrews 4:12 and Psalm 119:1-16)

Where there is a **DESIRE** for the gifts.	I Corinthians 12:31
Where there is **FAITH**.	Romans 12:6-7
Where there is a **HEART THAT SEEKS AFTER GOD**.	Acts 13:1-2
Where there is a **WILLINGNESS** to use the gift or ministry for the benefit of others.	Romans 12:6-7

THE PURPOSE OF THE GIFTS

To Perfect The Saints	Ephesians 4:11-13
To BUILD up the church.	I Corinthians 14:12
To PROTECT the church from sin.	Acts 5:8-9
To give WARNINGS to Christians.	Acts 21:11
To give DIRECTION to believers.	Acts 13:1-2

THE GIFTS ARE TO BE CONTROLLED

The gifts should never DISTRACT, but always ADD to a service.	I Corinthians 14:40
God is a not a God of confusion, but of peace.	I Corinthians 14:27
The gifts can be CONTROLLED.	I Corinthians 14:32

GIFTS OF THE HOLY SPIRIT
Page 6

ALL OF THE GIFTS SHOULD MAKE ONE CONSCIOUS OF THE PRESENCE OF GOD.

The Holy Spirit always moves according to God's purpose in the meeting and never brings confusion (I Corinthians 14:33).

Each believer should wait on the Lord and be fully edified before coming to church in order to be prepared for whatever the Holy Spirit wants them (you/us) to do in any service.

JESUS CHRIST IS THE SAME YESTERDAY, TODAY, AND FOREVER, Hebrews 13:8.

LET Jesus USE YOUR LIFE, TO GLORIFY The Father, John 15.

YIELD YOUR SPIRIT TO HIM NOW, Romans 12:1-2.

THE GIFTS OF THE HOLY SPIRIT
- REVIEW -

1. According to I Corinthians 12:11, who distributes the gifts of the Spirit?

2. Generally, how is the gift of the word of wisdom used?

    a.
    b.
    c.
    d.

3. Read and then explain in your own words what the gift of the word of knowledge is according to John 4:16-19, Acts 11:28, and Acts 21:11.

4. Is the gift of faith the same as the faith that saved you? Give scripture.

5. What is the gift of healing, and who gets the glory?

6. What is the gift of the working of miracles? Give scriptures.

    a.
    b.
    c.

7. Give the definition for the gift of discerning of spirits.

8. Briefly explain the gift of tongues and explain its purpose.

9. What does the gift of interpretation of tongues do for the church, and what is it equal to?

10. Name the gifts of ministry mentioned in I Corinthians 12:28-30 and Ephesians 4:11-13 and explain the purpose of these gifts to the church.

NOTES

LESSON - 8

SCRIPTURAL HEALING

SCRIPTURAL HEALING

INTRODUCTION

Divine healing is the POWER OF GOD to heal the sick in answer to believing prayer.

It is a GIFT of God to those who believe, just as salvation or the baptism with the Holy Spirit is a GIFT to those who believe.

We DO NOT receive healing because we are good or deserve it.

We receive healing because Jesus Christ paid for it at the whipping post, and it is ours for the asking if we believe, Isaiah 53:1-12. Prophesied, 750 years B C.

Christ has bore our griefs, carried our sorrows, was wounded for our transgressions, was bruised for our iniquities, and with His stripes we are healed, Isaiah 53:1-12 and I Peter 2:24.

SEVEN COMPOUND NAMES

In His redemptive relation to man, Jehovah has seven compound names which reveal Him as meeting every need of man from his lost state until the end.

Jehovah = The Eternal One, The Self-Existent One, who reveals Himself as, I AM. Exodus 3:14

Jehovah-Jireh =	Jehovah will......**PROVIDE**	Genesis 22:13-14
Jehovah-Rapha =	The Lord that...**HEALETH**	Exodus 15:26
Jehovah-Nissi =	Jehovah My.....**BANNER**	Exodus 17:15
Jehovah-Shalom =	Jehovah our....**PEACE**	Judges 6:24
Jehovah-Raah =	The Lord My....**SHEPHERD**	Psalm 23
Jehovah-Tsidkenu =	The Lord is our..**RIGHTEOUSNESS**	Jeremiah 23:6
Jehovah-Shammah =	The Lord is the..**ABIDING PRESENCE**	Ezekiel 48:35

Jehovah-Rapha, as it is given in the original scripture, implies that more than physical healing is in mind (Exodus 15:26).

Scripture indicates that the soul is in need of healing when we fail to keep the commandments of God (III John 1:2). Refer to the WORK OUT YOUR OWN SALVATION lesson.

JESUS PAID THE TOTAL PRICE, FOR THE TOTAL DELIVERANCE, FOR THE TOTAL PERSON.

SCRIPTURAL HEALING
Page 2

SOME OF THE THINGS THAT CAUSE SICKNESS

1. Intemperance, Proverbs 25:16 and Psalm 127:2.
2. Sin, John 5:5-14.
3. Disobedience and murmuring, Exodus 15:22-26.
4. Speaking against God's anointed, Numbers 12:1-15.
5. Satan, Job 1 and Job 2:7.

BELIEVING PRAYER

The effectual fervent prayer of the righteous man availeth much, James 5:16.

FAITH has always been the prerequisite for divine healing. Look at the many times Jesus healed while He was here on earth.

Scriptural examples:

The paralytic healed (Luke 5:17-20). Who had faith?
The centurion's servant healed (Luke 7:1-10). Who had faith?
The woman bowed together for 18 years (Luke 13:10-13). Who had faith?

OTHER METHODS, James 5:13-16.

"Is any sick among you? Let him call for the elders of the church; and LET THEM PRAY over him, anointing him with oil in the name of the Lord."

"Confess your faults one to another, and PRAY ONE FOR ANOTHER, that ye may be healed."

PULLING DOWN STRONGHOLDS

Basically all illness comes from Satan. He is the one who has come to steal, kill, and destroy (John 10:10).

"And I (Jesus) will give you (followers) the keys of the kingdom of heaven; and whatsoever you shall bind on earth shall be bound in heaven; and whatsoever you shall loose on earth shall be loosed in heaven" Matthew 16:19.

"Cast down imaginations and every high thing that exalteth itself against the knowledge of God, and bring into captivity every thought to the obedience of Christ" (II Corinthians 10:3-5).

THE GREAT COMMISSION; GO YE INTO ALL THE WORLD AND PREACH THE GOSPEL TO EVERY CREATURE, AND THESE SIGNS SHALL FOLLOW. MARK 16:15-20

How Do We Receive Healing?

Most Christians are unaware, that our Heavenly Father strongly desires, for us to be healed and that Jesus our Lord paid the price for us to be healed. Healing for the body and soul were provided for in the Old Testament and it was prophesized in the Old Testament, that healing would be provided for in the New Testament, by the stripes on Jesus' back.

Sometimes when we (you) are still a babe in Christ, God will heal and do many things for us (you) because we (you) are still a babe. But as we (you) get older in the Lord, we are expected to grow up, developing our faith through study and learning to trust God.

The book of Hebrews says, "But without faith, it is impossible to please Him, for he that comes to God must believe that He is, and that He is a rewarder of them (who-so ever) that diligently seek Him ". (Heb. 11:6)

Jesus in all four gospels, would ask a person, what do you want? After the person spoke what he or she believed Jesus could do, they received their healing. Paul's words agree with what Jesus said, in Romans 10:8-17, he said, that faith comes by hearing the Word, believing the Word and speaking forth the Word, through the mouth.

If you need healing in your body, we would suggest, that you review the lesson on prayer, where it talks about, How to Approach God and Taking a Stance of Faith. We urge you to read all of the scriptures you can concerning healing, and meditate on them. Review the Faith Helps in the back of this manual. Because the Holy Spirit will not work out of our head, we have to sift God's Word from the head to the heart. The devotional time will help you to do this. God told Joshua, "Meditate on My Word day and night so you will be a good success".

When you have reached an understanding in your heart, where there are no questions concerning whether are not God wants you healed, just like when you finally believed that God wanted you to be saved, then you are ready to pray for your healing.

A Sample Prayer

Dear Lord Jesus, I thank you for paying the price for my healing, by the stripes on your back. Thank you for loving me that much. I ask you to let your healing virtue flow from the top of my head to the tip of my toe and heal my (Name the condition by name). Thank you Father in Jesus name. Amen

SCRIPTURAL HEALING
- Review -

1. What is divine healing?

2. How and why do we receive divine healing?

3. What is the compound name for the Lord that healeth (scripture also)?

4. Is the body the only thing that needs healing?

5. Name five things that cause sickness (scripture also).

    a.

    b.

    c.

    d.

    e.

6. What is the prerequisite for divine healing?

7. Basically, where does illness come from (scripture also)?

8. Jesus came to destroy the works of the devil. What are His followers to do about the works of the devil?

    a.

    b.

    c.

I AM

I WAS REGRETTING THE PAST
AND FEARING THE FUTURE.

SUDDENLY MY LORD WAS SPEAKING.

"MY NAME IS, I AM" HE PAUSED.

I WAITED, HE CONTINUED.

WHEN YOU LIVE IN THE PAST
WITH ITS MISTAKES AND REGRETS,
IT IS HARD, I AM NOT THERE.

MY NAME IS NOT, I WAS.

WHEN YOU LIVE IN THE FUTURE
WITH IT'S PROBLEMS AND FEARS,
IT IS HARD, I AM NOT THERE.

MY NAME IS NOT, I WILL BE.

WHEN YOU LIVE IN THIS MOMENT,
IT IS NOT HARD, I AM HERE.

MY NAME IS, "I AM".

BY HELEN MALLICOAT

NOTES

LESSON - 9

THE FRUIT OF THE HOLY SPIRIT

NOTES ON - THE FRUIT OF THE SPIRIT

All of these Lessons are only, the Tip, of the subject they cover. (Iceberg) It will be up to each of you to continue to study and Grow in Grace and in the Knowledge of the Lord. This is part of Working Out Your Salvation on pages 73-76.

This study is like laying a foundation to a building. The Word says that you must count the cost before you start to build. Scripture also says, that God and your Lord and Savior Jesus and the Holy Spirit indwelling you, will help lay the foundation and build your SPIRITUAL HOUSE with Jesus being the CHIEF CORNER STONE. (Ephesians 2:20)

Building God's Word into your heart is also laying TREASURE up in Heaven. What you have when you get to Heaven will be connected to what you do with God's Word and His Son Jesus, before you go. (Matthew 6:19 & 33) The only thing you can take with you to Heaven is, the SPIRITUAL TREASURE you laid up there and the souls of people that through a joint effort of the body have helped to receive Jesus as their Personal Savior. This includes the local church and missionary efforts, all working together.

As we consider the FRUIT OF THE SPIRIT we must look at the CHARACTER and NATURE of God Himself. (Galatians 5:22-25) - Read the whole chapter and II peter I:2-11 on page 28) Jesus is the IMAGE of the Father. Our Father wants us to grow into the IMAGE of His Son Jesus. REMEMBER, our growth is PROGRESSIVE from the day we became born again until the day God takes us HOME. Snuggle - snuggle - snuggle.
So the FRUIT of the Spirit grows as we grow into the image of our God. Remember the Four Stages of Growth on page 13.

In II Peter 1:2-11, underline where it says, God gives us His own character. The Fruit of the Spirit in Galatians chapter 5, is representative of God's character and we can add to that, the Father's Agape Love in I Corinthians 13 and His capacity to forgive in John 3:1-21 and I John 1:9. Then we add chapter 15, The Vine and the Branches, which means being involved as co-laborers with God in the work of the Harvest. Jesus said, "How much more shall the Heavenly Father give the Holy Spirit to them that ask". Luke 11:13

This is DEVELOPING A PROGRESSIVE RELATIONSHIP with our Heavenly Father and Jesus our Lord.

THE FRUIT OF THE SPIRIT

INTRODUCTION

The true Christian life is characterized by the manifestation of certain virtues.

These true Christian virtues are, the FRUIT OF THE HOLY SPIRIT, not the fruit of human effort (Galatians 5:13-26). GOD HAS GIVEN US HIS VERY OWN NATURE. (II Peter 1:4)

Only when we are full of the Holy Spirit, do we exhibit a fruition of Christian virtues. (Acts 1:8 & 6:1-8 and John 7:37-39)

When Christ is FULLY FORMED in us, by the INDWELLING of the Spirit, TRUE CHRISTIAN VIRTUES WILL BE THE RESULT.

If there is no evidence of fruit in our life, we need to examine ourselves for a lack of understanding, of what God expects of us and has provided for us and the possibility of sin in our life.

Inasmuch as the Holy Spirit indwells the believer, we should expect to see this fruit in our lives as we grow in grace and knowledge of our Lord and Savior Jesus Christ.

When a Born-Again person receives the "fullness" of the Spirit, he/she does not bear a different kind of fruit but rather a GREATER ABUNDANCE AND PURER QUALITY of the same fruit.

The ultimate goal is a daily Spirit-filled life, abundant in the fruit of the Spirit. (II Corinthians 5:20 -- AMBASSADORS FOR CHRIST)

Christ is the true vine. God the Father is the husbandman.
The believers are the branches. JOHN 15:1-8

Those who have been born again are expected to go and SIN NO MORE, bringing forth fruit indicative of TRUE REPENTANCE (John 15:16).

If the branch (WE/YOU do) does bear some fruit, the Father prunes it in order that it (WE) will bear more fruit (John 15:2).

The fiery trials and tests are used by the Father as pruning and purging instruments to develop us into the image of Jesus. The Father dose not cause the trials, but through them, He helps us grow in maturity.
(James 1:1-17, I Peter 1:7, & 4:12-14 and Romans 8:26-39)

THE SPIRIT-FILLED LIFE IS A CONTINUAL **PROGRESSIVE GROWTH** IN GRACE AND FRUITFULNESS UNTIL THE LORD COMES TO TAKE HIS BRIDE HOME.

THE FRUIT OF THE SPIRIT
Page 2

THREE FRUITS OF INWARD CHARACTER

1. **LOVE:** A strong, ardent, tender, unconditional devotion to the well being of someone else (I Corinthians 13:1-13).

2. **JOY:** Emotional excitement, which produces a glad, happy, and content feeling.

3. **PEACE:** A state of quietness, rest, harmony, and security in the midst of turmoil, strife, and temptation.

THREE FRUITS IN EXPRESSION TOWARD MAN WITH A CHRIST-LIKE ATTITUDE

1. **LONGSUFFERING** (PATIENCE): To endure with the frailties, offenses, and provocations of others without resentment.

2. **GENTLENESS** (KINDNESS): A disposition to be gentle, soft spoken, kind, even-tempered, and refined in character and conduct.

3. **GOODNESS:** The state of being good, kind, virtuous, generous, and Christ-like in character.

THREE FRUITS IN EXPRESSION TOWARD GOD

1. **FAITHFULNESS:** The acting out of whole-hearted confidence, assurance, trust, and reliance on God and His Word Being faithful to your commitment.

2. **MEEKNESS** (HUMILITY): An attitude of the heart that reflects a disposition to be gentle and kind in negative situations.
   JESUS WAS MEEK, NOT WEAK.

   HE CONQUERED ALL OF THE POWERS OF SATAN.

3. **TEMPERANCE:** An inward strength to control the fleshly appetites and passions.

   NOTE: ACCORDING TO II PETER 1:1-11, GOD GIVES US HIS OWN CHARACTER AS WE PRESS CLOSE TO HIM.

   YOU ARE A WORK OF GRACE IN PROGRESS.

GALATIANS 5:13-26
(LIVING BIBLE)

13. For, dear brothers, you have been given freedom: not freedom to do wrong, but freedom to love and serve each other.

14. For the whole Law can be summed up in this one command: "Love others as you love yourself."

15. But if instead of showing love among yourselves you are always critical and catty, WATCH OUT! Beware of ruining each other.

16. I advise you to obey only the Holy Spirit's instructions. He will tell you where to go and what to do, and then you won't always be doing the wrong things your evil nature wants you to.

17. For we naturally love to do evil things that are just the opposite from the things that the Holy Spirit tells us to do; and the good things we want to do when the Spirit has His way with us are just the opposite of our natural desires. These two forces within us are constantly fighting each other to win control over us, and our wishes are never free from their pressures.

18. When you are guided by the Holy Spirit, you need no longer force yourself to obey Jewish laws.

19. But when you follow your own wrong inclinations your lives will produce these evil results: impure thoughts, eagerness for lustful pleasure,

20. idolatry, spiritism (that is, encouraging the activity of demons), hatred and fighting, jealousy and anger, constant effort to get the best for yourself, complaints and criticisms, the feeling that everyone else is wrong except those in your own little group--and there will be wrong doctrine,

21. envy, murder, drunkenness, wild parties, and all that sort of thing. Let me tell you again AS I HAVE BEFORE, THAT ANYONE LIVING THAT SORT OF LIFE WILL NOT INHERIT THE KINGDOM OF GOD.

22. But when the Holy Spirit controls our lives He will produce this kind of fruit in us: LOVE, JOY, PEACE, PATIENCE, KINDNESS, GOODNESS, FAITHFULLNESS,

23. GENTLENESS AND SELF-CONTROL; and here there is no conflict with Jewish laws.

GALATIANS 5:13-26
Page 2

24. Those who belong to Christ have nailed their natural evil desires to His cross and crucified them there.

25. If we are living now by the Holy Spirit's POWER, let us follow the Holy Spirit's LEADING in every part of our lives.

26. Then we won't need to look for honors and popularity, which lead to jealousy and hard feelings.

Galatians 6:7,

DON'T BE MISLED; REMEMBER THAT YOU CAN'T IGNORE GOD AND GET AWAY WITH IT. A MAN WILL ALWAYS REAP JUST THE KIND OF CROP HE SOWS.

Scripture quotations are taken from *The Living Bible,* copyright 1971. Used by permission of
Tyndale House Publishers, Inc. Wheaton, IL 60189 USA.
All rights reserved.

LESSON - 10

THE PATHWAY TO INNER PEACE

THE PATHWAY TO INNER PEACE
II PETER 1:2-11 & GALATIANS 5:13-26

Other than known sin and lack of faith, the greatest hindrance to prayer, is not knowing about the need to forgive others that have hurt us or the refusal on our part to do so.

In almost every teaching about prayer, Jesus concluded with the necessity to forgive others as the Father forgave us. There is a very specific reason why we should forgive others. Learning to forgive is for our benefit right now.

The other person or people may be unresponsive to our attempt to forgive them and to ask them to forgive us. Some people who have hurt us the deepest may have passed on. It is still very important that we choose to forgive them. Our Heavenly Father will help us in this decision and act of obedience. The main benefit of choosing to forgive is, it lets the Holy Spirit work from the inside out to do something the psychiatrist cannot do, which is to clean away anything that would hinder our relationship with the Father in Heaven.

We may find our self not wanting to forgive because the actions of others are still hurting us too much, and we may be so angry with them, we would like to do them bodily harm. However, if we will stop and listen to what our Lord is saying, He is telling us something that will reap benefits for us now and for eternity.

Hebrews 4:12 tells us, that God knows the thoughts and intent of the heart. So we must be open, honest and up front with the Lord and tell Him like it is. The Lord can see in every nook and cranny of our spirit and soul. He wants us to surrender all of the things that have hurt us, to Him, so that we can become spiritually healthy and emotionally strong.

The Holy Spirit washes away and heals all of the emotional damage that has occurred to us, from childhood to this present day, when we surrender those hurts to the Lord. Remember, the Holy Spirit is the only one that can and will work from the inside out.

Look unto Jesus, who is the author and finisher of our faith.
 (Hebrews 12:2) Jesus said in John 15:5, that without Him we can't do anything.

Paul said in II Corinthians 10:4-6, that we must discipline our thought life.

I Peter 5:7-11 says, to cast all of your care upon Jesus, because He cares for you.

Paul said in Hebrews 12:15, "do not to let the root of bitterness come in". The root of bitterness will develop into a big tree, which uproots all of the good things in your life.

THE PATHWAY TO INNER PEACE
Page 2

Sift God's word into your heart so you can eventually forgive others from your heart. Jesus will help you. Your growth is progressive.
Review, Romans 10:9-10

Jesus said while on the cross, "Father forgive them, they don't know what they are doing." Luke 23:34

Stephen said, when he was being stoned to death, "Lord don't charge them with this sin." Acts 7:60

Paul asked the Father to forgive the people who had wronged him.

Ask the Lord to help you to be willing to take the step of faith, to be released of all emotional damage that has occurred in your life. He is waiting for you to ask Him.

Start speaking out and say, "Father, in the name of Jesus your Son, I choose to obey your Word, so I forgive (name the person and situation) in the name of Jesus. Amen."

You may not feel a release the first time you pray this prayer, but if you continue in obedience to your Lord, you will be delivered from the hurts that oppress and hinder you.

The pathway to peace and joy is being forgiven of our sin, and learning to forgive others that have hurt us, and developing a personal relationship with our Lord and Savior. Review the lesson on, WORK OUT YOUR OWN SALVATION.

Review, "COME UNTO ME", WORDS TO REMEMBER, Stress or Peace of Mind and the other FAITH HELPS, in the back of this manual.

More scripture on learning to forgive: Matthew 6:14, Mark 11:22-26, Colossians 1:18 and 3:13, Ephesians 4:32, and I Corinthians chapter 13.

LET JESUS BE PREEMINENT IN YOUR LIFE.

A Special Note; This lesson is the shortest in this Seminar, and yet it is the most powerful resource to spiritual and mental health. When this principle is truly applied, you can have the true peace and joy that Jesus described in the gospels. If you find that you are still having a problem in this area of forgiving, we recommend finding a mature Christian counselor to assist you in this matter.

LESSON - 11

WORK OUT YOUR OWN SALVATION?

WORK OUT YOUR OWN SALVATION ?

Most people use different excuses not to get involved with the Bible and one of the most often excuses used is, MAN WROTE THE BIBLE AND THERE ARE TOO MANY MISTAKES AND CONTRADICTIONS IN IT.

HAVE YOU EVER THOUGHT THAT YOUR-SELF, OR HAVE YOU HEARD SOME-ONE SAY SOMETHING ON THAT ORDER?

After many years of Bible study, you will never find a mistake or contradiction anywhere in this precious book. The bible is comprised of 66 books, penned by 40 Holy Spirit controlled men over a 4000 year period. The Bible says this about it self in II Peter 1:20-21, "THE SCRIPTURE DID NOT COME BY THE WILL OF MAN, BUT HOLY MEN OF GOD AS THEY WERE MOVED BY THE HOLY SPIRIT."

The biggest MISTAKE OF ALL IS HOW MAN OVER THE YEARS HAS ATTEMPTED TO INTERPRET GOD'S WORD. GOD DID NOT INCLUDE INSTRUCTIONS ON HOW TO INTERPRET HIS WORD. HE LEFT INSTRUCTIONS ON HOW TO FOLLOW THE WORD LITERALLY AND TO BE LED BY HIS HOLY SPIRIT.

If we could take the time to go through the Old Testament, locating the 300 plus prophecies concerning the First coming of Jesus and then go to the New Testament and look up their fulfillment, it would not take a Rocket Scientist to recognize that man had NO PART IN WRITING THE BIBLE. Man has never had the capacity to project or look forward thousands of years into the future, record it and then fulfill it.

One of the assumed contradictions people use to support their claim that the Bible was written by man deals with the controversial question of, ARE WE SAVED BY GRACE? OR, ARE WE SAVED BY WORKS? This is the SUBJECT we would like to focus on in this lesson.

Paul said in Ephesians 2:8-9 that we are saved by GRACE NOT BY WORKS. Then Paul says in Philippians 2:12-16 THAT WE SHOULD WORK OUT OUR OWN SALVATION - WITH FEAR AND TREMBLING.

THESE VERSES WOULD APPEAR TO BE VERY CONTRADICTING STATEMENTS.

WHICH IS IT?

THE ANSWER TO THIS QUESTION HAS CAUSED MANY CHURCH SPLITS OVER THE YEARS AND IT IS THE REASON THAT THERE IS A WIDE SEPARATION IN CHURCH THEOLOGY TODAY. WE HAVE CHURCHES THAT ARE VERY LIBERAL AND WE HAVE CHURCHES THAT ARE VERY LEGALISTIC BASED ON THIS ISSUE.

ARE WE SAVED BY GRACE? OR, ARE WE SAVED BY WORKS?

THE ANSWER IS BOTH, BECAUSE THERE IS A PART THE FATHER, SON AND HOLY SPIRIT HAS DONE AND IS DOING AND THERE IS A PART THAT EACH OF US HAVE TO DO SINCE WE HAVE RECEIVED JESUS AS PERSONAL SAVIOR.

When we come to Jesus and are born-again, we become a new creature in Christ Jesus. We are cleansed from sin THROUGH JESUS' BLOOD. JESUS' BLOOD IS THE ONCE AND FOR ALL SACRIFICE FOR THE SIN OF ALL MANKIND (Hebrews 7:27).
Review; Hebrews chapters 7-9.

God has cast all our sin into, His sea of forgetfulness, never to remember our sin again (God's delete button). God will not and does not restore and remind us of what we did in the past. Romans 8:1 says, "Now therefore there is no more condemnation". We are absolutely and perfectly cleansed from sin the moment we receive Jesus as our Lord and Savior.

HERE LIES THE PROBLEM

We, through habitual lives, dirty ourselves again, with Satan's help. Paul asks the Galatians in chapter one and reminds them again in chapter 5:1-26, why, do you return to the things Jesus saved you from? The fleshly part of us DID NOT, become born again. OUR FLESH STILL WANTS TO KEEP DOING THE THINGS IT DID BEFORE WE CAME TO JESUS. (I Corinthians 9:27)

Refer to Romans 7:23 and I Corinthians 3:1-8.

We must GROW SPIRITUALLY to the point that our inner spirit, with the help of the Holy Spirit, FINALLY HAS CONTROL over the carnal (fleshly) part of us. I John 2:16 refers to, "The lust of the flesh, and the lust of the eyes, and the pride of life". Review the FOUR STAGES OF SPIRITUAL GROWTH on page 13.

THIS IS WHAT WORKING OUT YOUR OWN SALVATION IS ALL ABOUT. SIMPLY, GROWING UP SPIRITUALLY.

God says, "My people are destroyed BECAUSE OF THE LACK OF KNOWLEDGE" (Hosea 4:6). We can be born again and still be unlearned in regard to God's Word.
(I Corinthians 12:1 and 14:16 and 24).

There is still sin in the CARNAL (fleshly) part of us. That sin has to be dealt with, or we will be like the ten virgins, (five were not ready) we will not be ready when Jesus comes.

HOW CAN WE BE READY? BY APPLYING GOD'S WORD.

Romans 12:1-2 says, "Be ye transformed by the renewing of your mind." Psalms 119:11 says, "I hide your Word in my heart, so I will not sin against You." God said to Joshua in verse 1:8, "Meditate on My Word day and night, so you will be a good success." James 1:22 says, "be ye a doer of the Word, and not a hearer only."

The POWER IN GOD'S WORD, is more than enough, to help us maintain a life that is pleasing to our Lord, When we are shown sin in our life, WE NEED TO REPENT AND ASK GOD TO FORGIVE US AND NOT SIN ANY MORE, (I John 1:9) DON'T WAIT.

BUT GROW IN GRACE,
AND IN THE KNOWLEDGE OF OUR LORD
AND SAVIOR JESUS CHRIST.
TO HIM BE GLORY BOTH NOW
AND FOREVER. AMEN.

II PETER 3:18

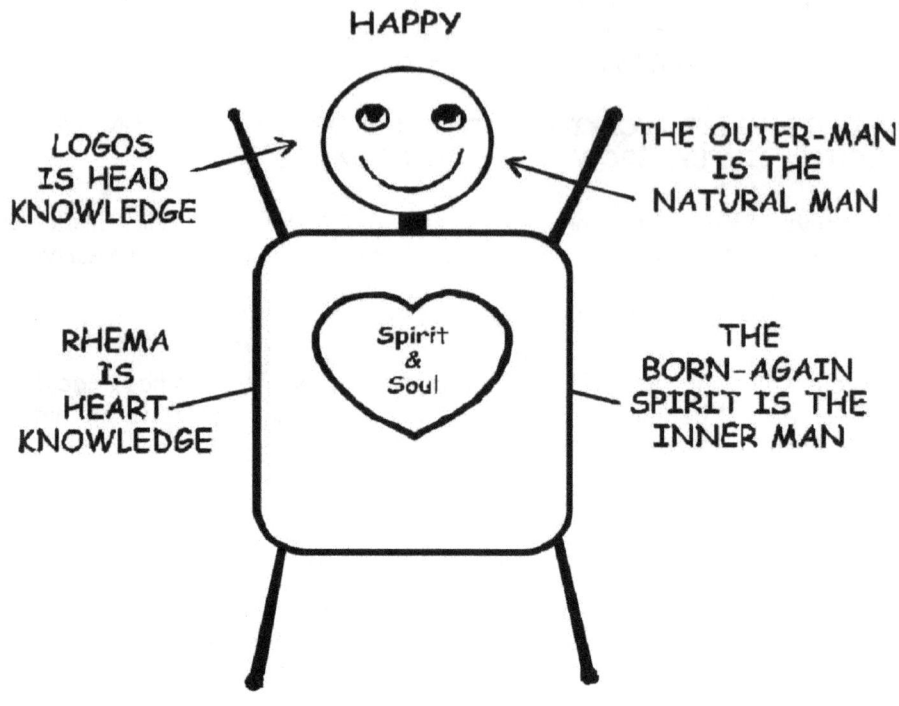

THE BIBLE SEPERATES THE NATURAL MAN FROM THE SPIRITUAL MAN. EPHESIANS 1:17-23 & EPHESIANS 3:16-20

THROUGH THE FOUR STAGES OF GROWTH, THE INNER MAN BECOMES STRONG ENOUGH TO TAKE CONTROL OVER THE NATURAL MAN AND STOPS HIM FROM SINNING.
2 CORINTHIANS 10:4-6 AND GALATIANS, CHAPTER 5

THE SPIRITUAL MAN LEARNING TO BE LED BY THE HOLY SPIRIT IS WHAT PAUL IS TALKING ABOUT WHEN HE SAYS, "WORK OUT YOUR OWN SALVATION." LESSON 11

GOD'S WORD APPLIED WILL WEAVE THE FABRIC OF FAITH INTO YOUR INNER SPIRIT. 2 PETER 3:18

LESSON - 12

CHRISTIAN WARFARE

CHRISTIAN WARFARE

When *PRIDE AND REBELLION CAME INTO SATAN'S HEART*, the *SPIRITUAL WARFARE BEGAN*. He was still a beautiful angel and the minister of music in heaven. He became impressed with how good and how beautiful he was and decided that he could take over God and His kingdom and rule the universe. He was able to convince one third of God's angels that his plan was POSSIBLE, so they too *REBELLED AGAINST GOD* and followed Satan.

Jesus said; "I saw Satan fall from Heaven". Jesus did not state when Satan fell, but it was probably about the time the *PLANS FOR CREATION* were being made or just before. This is why Satan was on the earth and was able to be in the garden to tempt Eve with the *FORBIDDEN FRUIT*.

JESUS SAID, "THE ENEMY HAS COME TO STEAL, KILL AND DESTROY, BUT I HAVE COME TO GIVE YOU ETERNAL LIFE".

Our enemy has at least 6000 years of experience in stealing, killing and destroying and in our *NATURAL CAPABILITIES, WE DO NOT STAND A CHANCE AGAINST HIM. BUT JESUS ALSO SAID, "CHEER UP, I HAVE OVER-COME THE WORLD".* Satan, was Jesus' *PRIMARY TARGET*, because, Satan is the father of lies and all of the evil he has been doing in this world, to come against God's plan. *All FOUR GOSPELS* are communicating *THE SPIRITUAL COMBAT* between Jesus and Satan.

Jesus *KNEW* that when He went home to the Father that His and our enemy would bring all of his forces to destroy the Church, which is also Jesus' Bride. He said the NIGHT OF THE LAST SUPPER, "I will not, leave you comfortless, (meaning, being left helpless against the enemy) but I will send the comforter, and when He, the Holy Spirit comes, He will do all these things for you". Jesus also said, *"GREATER IS HE THAT IS IN YOU THAN HE THAT IS IN THE WORLD".*

Jesus taught that the enemy was a *REAL FORCE* to contend with, He also taught that *HE, THE FATHER AND THE HOLY SPIRIT WOULD GIVE US THE RESOURCES TO BE MORE THAN CONQUERS.*

We have been given a *WORD PICTURE* in the Bible as to our *SPIRITUAL GROWTH*. Through this Seminar, we have been comparing Satan coming to destroy us in comparison to the Holy Spirit coming to build us up and Jesus having already paid the complete price for our *DELIVERANCE* and *ETERNAL LIFE.*

The Word Picture
Page 2

Satan steals, kills, destroys	Jesus builds us up
THE SOWER – MARK 4:1-20	THE FOUR STAGES OF GROWTH
1. THE WAY SIDE	1. THE BABE
2. THE STONY GROUND	2. THE CHILD
3. THE THORNY PLACES	3. THE YOUNG PERSON
4. THE GOOD GROUND	4. THE MATURE PERSON

James 1:1-27 says;

A DOUBLE MINDED MAN WILL NOT RECEIVE THE THINGS OF GOD.

BE YE A DOER OF THE WORD AND NOT A HEARER ONLY.

THE GREATER THE SPIRITUAL WARFARE, THE LARGER AMOUNTS OF GOD'S WORD IS NEEDED TO BE APPLIED TO THE INNER MAN, TO BRING DELIVERANCE AND VICTORY.

PRESENT YOUR BODY A LIVING SACRIFICE, HOLY, ACCEPTABLE UNTO GOD, WHICH IS YOUR REASONABLE SERVICE. AND BE NOT CONFORMED TO THIS WORLD, ROMANS 12:1-2.

FOR THE WEAPONS OF OUR WARFARE ARE NOT CARNAL, BUT MIGHTY THROUGH GOD, FOR THE PULLING DOWN OF STRONGHOLDS, II CORINTHIANS 10:3-7.

PUT ON THE WHOLE ARMOR OF GOD, EPHESIANS 6:10-18.

NOT BY MIGHT NOR BY POWER, BUT BY MY SPIRIT, SAITH THE LORD OF HOST, ZECHARIAH 4:6.

GREATER IS THE HOLY SPIRIT THAT IS IN YOU, THAN HE THAT IS IN THE WORLD, I JOHN 4:4.

CHRISTIAN WARFARE
Page 3

Read Colossians 3:1-17. IF YOU THEN, BE RISEN WITH CHRIST, SEEK THOSE THINGS WHICH ARE ABOVE, WHERE CHRIST SITS AT THE RIGHT HAND OF GOD.

SET YOUR AFFECTIONS ON THINGS ABOVE, Verse 2.

MORTIFY YOUR MEMBERS, (PUT TO DEATH) Verse 5.

1. Fornication
2. Uncleanness
3. Unrestrained affections
4. Carnal, illicit sexual desires or lust
5. Indulge in or have eager desires to acquire or attain things belonging to another (covetousness).
6. That which the affections are passionately set upon (idolatry).

PUT OFF, Verse 8.

1. Anger
2. Wrath
3. Malice
4. Blasphemy
5. Filthy communication
6. Lie not
7. The old man

PUT ON, Verse 10.

1. The NEW MAN after the image of Him that created man
2. Renew your mind
3. Bowels of mercy
4. Bowels of kindness
5. Humbleness of mind, meekness
6. Longsuffering
7. Forgiveness
8. Above all, LOVE
   Review; I Corinthians 13 and Galatians chapter 5.

LET THE PEACE OF GOD RULE in your hearts and let the Word of Christ **DWELL** in you richly in all wisdom (Verses 15-16).

CHRISTIAN WARFARE
page 4

EPHESIANS CHAPTER 6, Put on the WHOLE ARMOR of God, that you may be able to stand against the wiles of the devil.

1. Loins gird with truth. . . . . John 8:31-32 and 16:13
2. Breastplate of RIGHTEOUSNESS . . . . I Peter 2:24
3. Feet shod WITH THE GOSPEL OF PEACE . . Ephesians 6:15
4. Shield of FAITH . . . . I John 5:4
5. Helmet of salvation . . . . Acts 4:12
6. Sword of the spirit . . . . Hebrews 4:12
7. Pray always with all prayer and supplication IN THE SPIRIT
   Ephesians 6:18 and Romans 8:26-27

SPIRITUAL WEAPONS: II CORINTHIANS 10:3-5

"For though we walk in the flesh, we do not war after the flesh." "For the weapons of our warfare are not carnal but mighty through God to the pulling down of strongholds."

"Casting down imaginations and every high thing that exalteth itself against the knowledge of God and bringing into captivity every thought to the obedience of Christ."

THE CHRISTIAN'S FOES: EPHESIANS 6:12

1. Principalities . . . . The territory of a reigning (demonic) prince.
2. Powers . . . . Influences and demonical powers.
3. Rulers of Darkness . . . Anything contrary to God's rule.
4. Spiritual Wickedness. . The desire to take as many souls as possible
   to eternal hell (steal, kill, and destroy).

THE CHRISTIAN'S VICTORY: COLOSSIANS 2:9-15

In Christ dwelleth all the fullness of the Godhead bodily, and you are complete in Him, which is the Head of ALL PRINCIPALITY AND POWER.

1. Circumcised in your heart.
2. Buried with Christ in baptism.
3. Risen with Christ through faith.
4. Quickened together with Christ, having ALL your trespasses forgiven.
5. Christ broke the power of principalities and powers and made a show of them openly, triumphing over them.

GOD HAS DELIVERED US FROM THE POWER OF DARKNESS AND HAS RECREATED US INTO THE KINGDOM OF HIS DEAR SON. JESUS IS THE IMAGE OF THE INVISIBLE GOD, THE FIRSTBORN OF EVERY CREATURE.
COLOSSIANS 1:13-14

THE NEW COVENANT AUTHORITY

1. **MATTHEW 26:28:** "**For this is MY BLOOD OF THE NEW COVENANT.**"

Mark 9:23	"If you can believe, all things are possible."
Mark 10:27	"With God all things are possible."
Mark 11:22-26	"If you say unto this mountain . . ."
Hebrews 7:12-28; 8:1	Jesus is the once and for all sacrifice.

2. **REVIEW JESUS' AUTHORITY**

Matthew 4:1-11	Jesus overcame the enemy with the Word.
Luke 4:1-13	Jesus overcame the enemy with the Word.
Luke 7:18-23	Jesus came to set the captives free.
Matthew 28:18	All POWER is given unto Jesus.
Acts 10:38	God anointed Jesus, with the Holy Spirit.
Colossians 1:9-23	Jesus is the HEAD OF THE CHURCH.

3. **LOOK AT THE RESULTS OF PEOPLE NOT READY FOR SPIRITUAL COMBAT**

Acts 19:1-19	The seven brothers.

4. **LOOK AT THE AUTHORITY DELEGATED TO US THROUGH JESUS' DIRECT COMMAND**

Matthew 28:19-20	"Go ye into all the world . . ."
Mark 13:34-37	Jesus gave authority to His servants.
Mark 16:14-20	Jesus worked with the disciples.
Luke 10:19	Jesus gave the church power to tread on the enemy.
Colossians 1:1-29	Read this entire chapter, but look at verse 13 for what it is really saying.

THE PRAYER OF BINDING AND LOOSING
Page 1

1. **NOT BY OUR POWER BUT BY THE POWER IN JESUS' NAME**

    a. Jesus gave us the keys (Matthew 16:17-19; 18:18-20).
    b. Read Mark 16:14-20.
    c. Read Colossians 1:9-23.
    d. Not by might, not by power, but by my Spirit says the Lord" (Zechariah 4:6).
    The Book of Acts study helps us see this truth in action.

2. **COME TOGETHER - AGREE IN ONE ACCORD - HOW CAN TWO WALK TOGETHER UNLESS THEY AGREE WITH ONE ANOTHER?**

    a. This applies to the fact that when we FINALLY say to the Father, "Father, you know what you are doing, and I choose to do it your way."
    b. The Lord says, "Come, let us reason together" Isaiah 1:18.

3. **GIVE THANKS ALWAYS TO THE FATHER, EPHESIANS 5:20.**

    a. Look at the situation through God's eyes (II Corinthians 10:3-7).
    b. This situation is an opportunity for God to use you, to DO a MIRACLE, to bless you, and to bring honor and glory to Himself.

4. **WHATEVER WE ASK IN JESUS' NAME OUR FATHER WILL DO IT (JOHN 16:23)**

    a. We have direct access to the Father under the New Covenant.
    b. Review THE NIGHT OF THE LAST SUPPER.

5. **MEDITATE ON GOD'S WORD DAY AND NIGHT (JOSHUA 1:8)**

    a. God has a way to transform us (Romans 12:1-2).
    b. We must speak from the heart, not the head (Romans 10:9-10).
    c. Our mountain CAN BE MOVED (Mark 11:22-26).

6. **WE MUST ACCEPT, TAKE, AND USE THE AUTHORITY GIVEN US BY JESUS OUR LORD**

    a. Be a doer of the Word (James 1:22).
    b. Review THE NEW COVENANT AUTHORITY.

THE PRAYER OF BINDING AND LOOSING
Page 2

6. **OPPOSITION IS NORMAL - YOU MUST STAND YOUR GROUND, ESPECIALLY IN YOUR THOUGHT LIFE (II CORINTHIANS 10:1-6)**

    a. We are told not to fight one another in Ephesians 6:10-18.

    b. Fight the GOOD FIGHT OF FAITH in I Timothy 6:12.

    c. Our hardest fight is in OUR THOUGHT LIFE as taught in II Corinthians 10:5.

    d. DO what God's Word says; don't waiver in James 1:1-9.

    e. BE SPECIFIC IN YOUR PRAYER.

    NAME NAMES, ILLNESSES, PLACES, ETC.

Example

IN THE NAME OF JESUS CHRIST, I BREAK THE POWER

(Be specific)

OF SATAN OVER MY FAMILY, FRIENDS, AND NEIGHBORS

AND CLAIM THEIR DELIVERANCE AND SALVATION.

AMEN!

BINDING AND LOOSING
IN DAILY RELATIONSHIPS

1. Your attitude: Do you walk in love or with a chip on your shoulder? (I Corinthians chapter 13)

2. Are the decisions you make based on Biblical facts or hearsay?

3. Is the stance you take based on your own decision?

4. Action taken - James 1:22 teaches us to be a doer of the word and not a hearer only Look at Romans 12:1-21.

5. You can bind or loose life - Galatians chapter 5 ("walk in the spirit" and Romans 14:17-18).

6. You can bind or loose death - Acts Ch. 5 (Sapphira and Ananias).

7. You can bind and loose joy - Galatians chapter 5, the fruit of the Spirit.

8. You can bind and loose sorrow - James 3:1-6 (tongue and actions). also Galatians chapter 5.

9. **BINDING AND LOOSING EQUALS, WHAT YOU HAVE ESTABLISHED, IN YOUR HEART, THOUGHTS, WORDS AND ACTIONS.**

10. Hebrews 4:12: **THE WORD OF GOD IS SHARP AND POWERFUL.**

11. II Corinthians 10:3-6: **BRING EVERY THOUGHT UNTO OBEDIENCE.**

12. Romans 12:1-2: **PRESENT YOUR BODIES A LIVING SACRIFICE, AND PRESENT YOUR (SPEECH) TONGUES AS A LIVING SACRIFICE ALSO.**

LESSON – 13

LEARNING TO SHARE GOD'S LOVE

LEARNING TO SHARE GOD'S LOVE

INTRODUCTION:

The Apostles did not, originally, comprehend the breadth of the "Great Commission" given to them by Jesus in Matthew 28:19-20. They sought to establish a Jewish Christian Church consisting of converted Jews and Jewish proselytes.

Later, through the enlightening influence of the Holy Spirit they recognized the universality of the Gospel call, and admitted Gentiles into full fellowship. Acts chapter 15

Jesus' last words were, "Ye shall receive power after the Holy Spirit has come upon you to be my witness".

The responsibility of proclaiming the GOOD NEWS about Jesus has been given directly to the BODY OF CHRIST, which we are when we become Born-Again.

The Angels Of God are not able to take this Message of God's LOVE to the world. They are sometimes given assignments to assist in the work of the Body of Christ fulfilling their assigned task.

In Acts chapter two, we read about Peter's first opportunity to preach. Three thousand people gave their lives to Christ because of what Peter said under the POWER OF THE HOLY SPIRIT.

About nine years later the Holy Spirit gave Peter a vision to wash out his prejudices toward the gentile people, and sent Peter to the house of Cornelius. All that lived in this house received Jesus as their personal Savior, as a result of Peter, being obedient to the leading of the Holy Spirit.

In chapter nine we read about the conversion of Paul, how God gave him a vision and a visitation of Jesus to correct all of the learning he had received going to the religious seminary. Paul wanted to be a servant of God with all his heart, but, he was going about it the wrong way. Paul himself, had to be converted and receive Jesus as personal savior.

Paul's ministry and missionary work covered about twenty-seven years. He was put into prison for preaching the gospel. It was while in prison, Paul wrote the letters to the churches and these letters are now the larger part of the New Testament as we know it today.

It is an AWESOME PRIVILEGE and RESPONSIBILITY, the Lord has given us. Shall we PRAY that we too, SHALL CATCH GOD'S VISION, THAT HE IS NOT WILLING ANY SHOULD PERISH, and we WILL DO OUR PART, that those we come in CONTACT WITH, WILL HEAR FROM OUR MOUTH AND SEE, THROUGH OUR LIFE-STYLE, THAT WE SERVE, THE ONE AND ONLY TRUE LIVING GOD. II Peter 3:9

SALVATION PREACHING
THE CROSS AND THE RESURRECTION, WATER BAPTISM AND THE BAPTISM IN THE HOLY SPIRIT

In all four Gospels, Jesus is the ROLE MODEL. He begins with the twelve Apostles, teaching, training and grooming. Then He sends them out two by two. Then He sends seventy others out two by two. For three years Jesus is preparing the leaders He is going to leave behind to do the Father's WORK and to prepare His Bride.

THEN JESUS SAID TO THE CHURCH: "AS THE FATHER SENT ME, SO SEND I YOU." This command is still in effect today.

HERE ARE SOME EXAMPLES:

1. John the Baptist, Preached repentance and to look for the coming of Jesus. (The Messiah)

2. John 3:3; Jesus told Nicodemus: "YOU MUST BE BORN-AGAIN"

3. John 4:5-30: Jesus taught about the LIVING WATER

4. John 14:6: Jesus said, "He was THE WAY, THE TRUTH, AND THE LIFE."

5. Acts 2:38-39; Then Peter said unto them: "Repent, and be baptized every one of you, in the name of Jesus Christ for the remission of sins, and you shall receive the gift of the Holy Spirit. For the promise is unto you, and to your children, and to all that are afar off, even as many as the Lord our God shall call."

6. Acts 3:17-24; "Yea, and all the prophets from Samuel and those that follow after, have foretold of these days."

7. Acts 4:12; "Neither is there salvation in any other; for there is none other name under heaven given among men, whereby we must be SAVED."

8. Acts 8:26-40; Philip and the Eunuch

9. Acts 9:1-22; The conversion of Saul

10. Acts 10:1-48; Cornelius and his house

11. Acts 13:26; Paul said, "Men and brethren, children of the stock of Abraham, and whosoever among you (GENTILES) WHO FEARETH God, to you is the WORD of SALVATION SENT."

12. Acts 20:20 could be called, **"Gods VISION"** of how He wants His church to VIEW, " THE WORK OF THE HARVEST".
    Look at Matthew 9:37-38

LEARNING TO SHARE GOD'S LOVE
Page 1

1. OUTLINE OF GODS REASON FOR SENDING JESUS.

    A. Luke 19:10 & Ezekiel 34:11-16 To SEEK and to SAVE that which was LOST.

    B. Luke 4:14-21 To SET the CAPTIVES FREE

    C. Luke 7:18-23 To SET the CAPTIVES FREE

    D. Isaiah 58:6 To SET the CAPTIVES FREE

    E. John 3:16 For God so LOVED the world that HE SENT JESUS (His Son).

    F. John 3:17 Jesus Came to SAVE the world and NOT to CONDEMN THE WORLD.

    G. Acts 10:38 God anointed Jesus with the Holy Spirit and with POWER, TO SET THE CAPTIVES FREE.

2. THE CHAIN OF COMMAND.

    A. John 20:21 "As the FATHER sent ME, so SEND I YOU"

    B. II Tim. 2:15 We are instructed to study.

    C. Rom. 10:17 FAITH comes by hearing.

    D. John 16:1-33 THE PERSON OF THE HOLY SPIRIT was SENT to GUIDE, LEAD and TEACH US.

    E. Luke 4:1-13 Jesus OVERCAME the enemy WITH THE WORD. Matt 4:1-11

    F. Rev. 12:11 We OVERCOME the enemy by the BLOOD OF THE LAMB and by our testimony, connected TO THE WORD.

    G. Mark 16:14-20 Jesus works with us and confirms the WORD. Look at verses 19 & 20 also Isaiah 55:11.

    H. Acts 1:8 **Go into all the world, BEGINNING in YOUR own NEIGHBORHOOD.**

LEARNING TO SHARE GOD'S LOVE
Page 2

3. THE PART WE DO

- A. I Peter 3:15 — Be ready to give an answer
- B. Acts 1:8 — You shall be witnesses
- C. I Cor. 4:6-11 — We are LABORERS together with God
- D. II Cor. 5:14-21 — We are AMBASSADORS for Christ
- E. II Tim. 1:7 — Live a SPIRIT-FILLED life (Eph. 5:18)
- F. Joshua 1:8 — Meditate (absorb, commit to memory) on God's WORD so you will be a GOOD SUCCESS.
- G. Psalms 107:1-2 — Give thanks unto the Lord, and let the redeemed say so!

4. GOD'S CONTINUED ATTITUDE

- A. II Peter 3:9 — He is NOT WILLING that ANY SHOULD PERISH
- B. I Tim. 2:3-5 — God would have all men SAVED
- C. Luke 15:10 — ALL HEAVEN REJOICES when one PERSON repents, THIS PLEASES OUR Heavenly FATHER.
- D. John 15:8 — Our Father is GLORIFIED
- E. Luke 14:23 — Go and COMPEL them to come in
- F. Matt. 9:37,38 — Pray to the Lord of the harvest
- G. Isaiah 6:8 — Here FATHER, here am I, SEND ME
- H. Ezekiel 3:17-21 — **READ THESE VERSES IF YOU ARE NOT SURE, HOW GOD FEELS ABOUT THIS SUBJECT.**

THE FIVE PHASES OF SOUL WINNING

INTRODUCTION: A person won to Christ usually has had previous work done in his life. There are exceptions, but generally speaking this previous history in contact can be found if we investigate. This study will analyze the before and after work with souls.

1. **PLOWING** – I Corinthians 9:10 "... he that ploweth should plow in hope." This is cultivation, when a Christian makes a favorable impression on a non-Christian by a good turn, sweet conduct under pressure, consistent godliness in an ungodly atmosphere, etc.

2. **PLANTING** – John 4:37 "one soweth and another reapth." Plowed ground can take the seed and the seed is the WORD OF GOD. Psalms 126:5 "He that goweth forth and weepeth, bearing precious seed …. This is another term given to this aspect is "sowing".

3. **WATERING** - I Corinthians 3:6-8 "I have planted and Apollos watered." This follows seed planting, and includes the calling, sharing truth, prayer, travail (with pangs), etc. Sometimes this involves years and sometimes only days or weeks.

4. **REAPING** – John 4:36 "He that reapeth recieveth wages." This is the act of winning a soul to Christ. Before you dealt with the person, he or she was a sinner. After you dealt with him or her, that one was a child of God – whether at the moment of dealing or later at church or at home alone, your persuasion brought the act.

5. **THRESHING** – I Corinthians 9:10 " ... and that he that thresheth in hope." This is follow-up when the genuine wheat in a person is separated from the chaff. (It can be "removing of grave cloths" John 11:44) Follow-up is often the most difficult part of the process and most exacting.

HOW ABOUT REWARDS?

"--- and every man shall receive his own reward according to his own labor" I Corinthians 3:8. The amount of effort, labor and time put into a person determine the amount of reward received.

HOW ABOUT WAGES?

"And he that reapeth, receiveth wages and gathereth fruit unto life eternal" John 4:36. "Wages" is given to the one who actually wins the soul, just as the farmer who reaps the field gets the crop. He has benefit from the life of the person won and also shares in his souls. Christ reaped the women at the well, she told the town and her converts invited Him and His team to stay and they stayed there two days. "And more believed because of His own word. " More converts (wages) came as a result of this one convert.
John 4:39-42

LESSON BY--CHRISTIANS IN ACTION , LONG BEACH, CA.

EVANGELISM -THOUGHTS

1. **CONSIDER THE VALUE GOD HAS PLACED ON EACH PERSON.**

    A. Each person is worth, more than all of the world and all the things there in. "What does it profit a person, if they gain the whole world, and then loose their soul".

2. **JESUS SAID: " I WILL MAKE YOU FISHERS OF MEN."**

    A. We need to learn how to use, different types of BAIT, for the DIFFERENT TYPES OF FISH.

3. **Ask some qualifying questions** such as: What would you say is man's greatest spiritual need? -or- What does a person need to do to go to Heaven? -or- How could you guarantee that you will go to Heaven when you die?

    When a person says, "I've been asked that before, or I have thought about that before."

    Then ask: What was your response to the question then, and how do you feel now?

    Wait for their response. Their answer will tell you where they are spiritually at this time.

4. **A thought about body language:** It is about 55% of how your communication impacts the person you are talking to.

5. If the opportunity is there... *DON'T LET IT PASS THEM BY. DON'T WASTE IT!* Then say -

    Would you like to ask Jesus into your heart to be your Personal Lord and Savior?

6. **WAIT ON THEIR ANSWER.**

7. Do not force a person for an answer. You can BRUISE THE FRUIT by forcing and NO ONE will be able to HARVEST it later. The Holy Spirit is a perfect gentleman, He never forces Himself on anyone.

The only thing we can do as workers is, PRAY, SOW SEEDS AND WATER, THE HOLY SPIRIT GIVES THE INCREASE. I Cor. 3:1-15.

THE TOP TEN EXCUSES

EXCUSE #1 "I can't live the Christian life."

ANSWER: Have you let the true source of POWER come into your HEART? John 1:12 "But as many as received Him, to them, gave He power, to become sons of God, even to them that believe on His name."

EXCUSE #2 "I will accept Jesus later."

ANSWER: You are only one, heart beat from eternity. James 4:14 "whereas ye know not what shall be on the morrow. For what is your life? It is even a vapor, that appeareth for a little time, and then vanisheth away."

EXCUSE #3 " I have my own religion."

ANSWER: What would happen if each person set his own traffic rules. Isaiah 53:6 says, "All we like sheep have gone astray; we have turned every one to his own way; and the Lord hath laid on JESUS, the iniquity of us all."

EXCUSE #4 "All religions are good."

ANSWER: But only Jesus rose from the dead. John 14:6 " Jesus saith to him, I am the way, the truth, and the life; no man cometh unto the Father but by me."

EXCUSE #5 " I go to church."

ANSWER: While attending church, have you ever received the gift of eternal life? Romans 6:23 " For the wages of SIN is death, but the gift of God is eternal life; through JESUS CHRIST our Lord."

TOP TEN EXCUSES-Cont.

EXCUSE #6 "I'll make it by my good works."

ANSWER: Then Jesus' death was a horrible mistake. Ephesians 2:8,9 "For by grace are ye saved through faith; and that not of yourselves: it is the gift of God: Not of works, lest any man should boast."

EXCUSE #7 "God doesn't have time for me."

ANSWER: He took time while dying to save a thief. Romans 5:8 says, "But God commendeth his love toward us, in that, while we were yet sinners, Christ died for us."

EXCUSE #8 "When you're dead you go six feet under and that is it"

ANSWER: Yes, that's where the body goes but-- how about the soul? Luke 16:22-23 says, "And it came to pass, that the beggar died and was carried by the angels into Abraham's bosom: the rich man also died, and was buried -AND IN HELL he lift up his eyes, being in torment, and seeth Abraham afar off, and Lazarus in his bosom."

EXCUSE #9 "There are too many hypocrites in the church."

ANSWER: Agreed! But would you throw a good $10 dollar bill away because you received a counterfeit one? Matthew 13:30 "Let both grow together until the harvest: and in the time of harvest I will say to the reapers, "Gather ye together first the tares, and bind them in bundles to burn them, but gather the wheat into my barn."

EXCUSE #10 "The Bible has too many errors."

ANSWER: Here is my Bible; will you show me one? 11 Timothy 3:16 SAYS, "All scripture is given by inspiration of God, and is profitable for doctrine, for reproof, for correction, for instruction in righteousness."

THE SIX STEP APPROACH

STEP 1

Soul Winner: "Do you ever give much thought to spiritual things?"

Response: "Oh, I guess I have. Not as much as I ought to though."

Step II

Soul Winner: "What would you say is man's greatest spiritual need?"

Response: "Oh, I don't know; going to church and believing in God I guess."

Step III

Soul Winner: God tells us, a man's greatest spiritual need is, an experience called, Being Born-again. Which means being forgiven of, all our sins, and receiving God's Gift of Eternal Life. Was there ever a time in your life when you seriously thought about your need of God's Gift?

Response: Oh, sure, just about everyone has.

Step IV

Soul Winner: What would you say a person should do to receive, God's Gift of Eternal Life?"

Response: Well, I'd say to believe in God and do the best you can."

Step V

Soul Winner: Yes you're right. Everyone ought to do those things. What I really had in mind was, how do WE go about receiving, God's Gift of Eternal Life?

Response: Usually, None.

Step VI

Soul Winner: Would it be all right if I shared a few verses of scripture with you? Together we can see what God has to say in regard to receiving, His Gift of ETERNAL LIFE.

THE SIX STEP APPROACH
Page 2

NOTE: The response here, is important, (do not push) be sensitive to the Holy Spirit..

Step VI, Response continued.

If the person says no. I do not want to talk about this now. You must respect their position at this time.
- Do not be pushy.
- Do not communicate your disappointment.
- Continue to be courteous to them.
- Thank them for their time and for listening to you.
- Put them on your Prayer list for people to be saved.

If the response is Yes.

- Simply pull out one of your brochures and share God's Truth with them.
- Be sure to have gotten their name so you can make John 3:16, personal to them as shown in the Brochure.
- When you are done sharing and answering the persons questions-
- Then say to them, Would you like to ask Jesus in to your heart to be your Personal Savior.
- If the answer is Yes;
- Ask the person if you may lead them in prayer to ask Jesus to be their Savior
- If the response is yes, then say; let's bow our head and you may follow me in prayer.
- You may use the prayer that is in the brochure or one that you are more comfortable with.
- When you are done praying, congratulate them on becoming a New Christian and for Becoming a brother or sister in the Lord.
- Be sure to get their name, address and phone number so you can do follow up and get them into church. They are a NEW Babe in Christ, and it is important to follow up on them.

Remember;

All of Heaven will be REJOICING with you, because of what has just taken place.   Amen!

LESSON - 14

WATER BAPTISM

WATER BAPTISM

1. **What is Water Baptism?**

   a. Water Baptism is an outward manifestation of an inward work of Grace (Being Born-Again).
   b. Water Baptism is the New Believer's first step of faith.
   c. Water Baptism is a Biblical church ordinance.

2. **Why should you be baptized?**

   a. You should be baptized because it is the first step of obedience. (Acts 2:38, Acts 2:41 and Matthew 28:19)
   b. You should be baptized because of the example of Christ.
      - Jesus was baptized to fulfill all righteousness. Matthew 3:15
      - Here He revealed Himself as the predicted Messiah. The ONE bringing righteousness to His people, fulfilling Old Testament prophecy.
      - Jesus was baptized to publicly announce the beginning of His ministry. (Levitical priest at age 30 were immersed in water, Exodus 29:4-7). First cleansing then anointing.
   c. We should be baptized because of the example of the early church.
      - It was the accepted pattern to repent and be baptized in water.
      - Philip baptized the Ethiopian eunuch. Acts 8:35-39
      - The House of Cornelius. Acts 10:47-48
      - Paul explains Water Baptism in Romans 6:3-10.
   d. We should be baptized to tell the world that we are Christians.
      - We are identifying with the DEATH, BURIAL and RESURRECTION of our LORD and SAVIOR - JESUS CHRIST.
   e. Being baptized identifies with Christ's death, burial, and resurrection.
      - Christ took our place at Calvary. He took our punishment. God placed our sins on Jesus at Calvary. Paul says in Galatians 2:20, "I am crucified with Christ; nevertheless I live; yet not I but Christ liveth in me."
   f. We should be baptized to have a good conscience before God.
      - Baptism is simply obedience to our Heavenly Father. We know we have done all that God requires up to this point. Our conscience should be at peace. (I Peter 3:21)

WATER BAPTISM
Cont.

- We cannot gain merit before God because salvation is by grace through faith in what Jesus did for us on the cross.
  - Baptism cannot add to our salvation, nor secure it.
  - Baptism cannot illuminate salvation so you can understand it.
  - Baptism cannot magnify our salvation so we can better serve Him.

Public confession through water baptism usually strengthens a new believer and brings joy and peace knowing we have obeyed Christ's Commandment.

3. **Why should you be baptized in *WATER* ?**

   a. Levitical priest at age 30 years were immersed in water. Water Baptism symbolized cleansing before the anointing. Exodus 29:4-7
   b. Jesus was baptized in water, like the Levitical priests, to publicly announce the beginning of His ministry.
   c. It was the accepted pattern of the early church to repent and then be baptized in water.
   d. Paul explains Water Baptism in Romans 6:3-10.

4. **Who should not be baptized?**

   a. People that are NOT BORN AGAIN.
   b. Little children and those incapable of making intelligent decisions are safe in God.
   (II Samuel 12:23 and Mark 10:14)

How should you get ready for water baptism?

- Check and verify the location, date and time.
- Bring a towel and a change of clothing.
- When it is your turn enter the water slowly.
- Be ready to give a word of testimony.
- Cross arms on your chest. (This is a symbol of death)
- Hold your nose as a protection.
- Bend knees and yield yourself to the one baptizing you.
- Watch your footing as you come up out of the water.

Note: Pictures may be taken during your baptism by a member of the family or a friend.

WATER BAPTISM
-REVIEW-

1. What is Water Baptism?

2. What are some of the reasons you should be baptized?

3. Why should you be baptized in WATER ?

4. Who should not be baptized?

5. Quote from memory Acts 2:38

NOTES

LESSON – 15

HOLY COMMUNION

HOLY COMMUNION

INTRODUCTION: Holy Communion is one of two ordinances given to the church by the Lord Jesus Christ. Water Baptism is the first one.

1. **What is an Ordinance?**
    a. Webster says it is, "an established rule, rite or law".
    b. Water Baptism and Holy Communion are ordinances established by Jesus before He left this earth to go home to the Father
    c. Remember the principal value of a parable.

2. **What is the purpose of Holy Communion?**
    a. To commemorate the death of our Lord Jesus Christ.
    b. To receive anew the benefits of the broken body and shed blood of our Lord Jesus.
    c. To enjoy the fellowship of the Lord's presence with other Christians.
    d. To be obedient to our Father's request.

3. **How often should we observe the Ordinances of Water Baptism and Holy Communion?**
    a. Water baptism is observed only once at the beginning of the Christian life. (Refer to the Water Baptism Study)
    b. Holy Communion is observed whenever Christians desire to have special fellowship and communion with the Lord and with other Christians. ("Do this in remembrance of Me" Luke 22:19)

4. **A brief look at the Old Testament Passover.**
    a. The Passover was a Jewish feast to commemorate the deliverance of Israel from the bondage in Egypt. Exodus Ch.12.
    b. The blood of the lamb over the door post was their deliverance from the death angel. Only the blood could save them.
    c. This was a type of Jesus, **THE LAMB OF GOD**, giving Himself for a once and for all sacrifice, that whosoever could be cleansed from **SIN**. This is also one of the 300 plus prophecies concerning the first coming of Jesus. Hebrews 7:27.

5. **The New Testament Passover.**
    a. John 1:29 introduces us to **THE LAMB OF GOD** who takes away the **SIN** of all who will come to God through His only begotten Son through faith.
    b. We must apply the Blood of Jesus to the doorpost of our heart along with asking for forgiveness in order to be cleansed from sin and receive eternal life. We do that by faith, when we take communion.

Refer to lesson #1, Acts 2:22-41, Isaiah 53:7, I Peter 1:18-19 and Rev. 13:8

HOLY COMMUNION
Cont.

5. The LORD'S LAST SUPPER

Jesus being a Jew, observed the Passover of the Old Testament with His disciples in Luke 22:7-13. Jesus was aware that this would be the last time He would partake of the Passover Feast with His disciples. His desire was that His followers would remember all that He had taught them, especially that He was giving His life for them, so they could stand before God in all pureness, washed from all their sins.

    a. Luke 22:14-20 shows us where Jesus used the Passover Feast communion to transition into the New Covenant. Jesus established Holy Communion as an ordinance. Also Mark 14:24 and Matthew 26:28

    b. John 6:33 tells us who the Bread of Life is and where it came from.

    c. Jesus said that the **BROKEN BREAD** represented His body. In the garden of Gethsemane He suffered so much agony that He sweat as it were, great drops of blood. (Psalms 107:20)

Jesus was beaten, crowned with thorns, spit upon, and His very beard was plucked out.

The cruel treatment on the cross was another way His body was broken, so we could receive eternal life.

    d. Three things we can receive by **FAITH** when we partake of Holy Communion are, **HEALING, STRENGTH AND DIVINE HEALTH.**

    e. The **ELEMENT** of the "CUP", represent, **CLEANSING, REMISSION, CANCELLATION** and **FORGIVENESS OF OUR SINS.**
      (Hebrews 9:11-28 and Psalms 103:1-22)

7. In ancient times people usually entered into most of their agreements by signing them with blood. These were then called blood covenants.

    a. Exodus 24:8 tells about the covenant God made with the children of Israel. God made His conditions known and the people agreed with them.

    b. I Corinthians 11:23-30 tells us what the conditions are for being New Covenant partakers of Holy Communion.

    c. We should have a right relationship with God, through Jesus Christ His Son.

    d. We should examine ourselves and confess any known sin **BEFORE we receive HOLY COMMUNION.** I Corinthians 11:20-34 & I John 1:9

HOLY COMMUNION-REVIEW

1. What is an ORDINANCE?

    a.

2. What is the purpose of Holy Communion?

    a

    b

    c

    d

3. How often should we observe Water Baptism and Communion?

    a

    b

4. What scripture introduced us to the Lamb of God, and who is HE?

5. When Jesus introduced the Elements of the Bread and the Cup to the Disciples for the first time, what was He trying to get them to understand?

6. What did the Broken Bread represent?

7. What did the Cup represent?

8. Name two of the conditions required for being a partaker of HOLY COMMUNION.

    a

    b

NOTE: **Memorize I John 1:9**

NOTES

LESSON - 16

SO WHAT ABOUT TITHING?

SO, WHAT ABOUT TITHING?

In Genesis chapter 4, God established the system of tithing and offerings as a means of keeping balance and accountability with mankind. The balance desired and the benefits achieved were not for God's benefit, but for man's benefit. God's motives have always been in the best interest of the mankind He created and loves.

God said in Jeremiah 29:11-14, "For I know the thoughts that I think toward you, saith the Lord, thoughts of peace and not of evil, to give you an expected end. Then shall you call upon Me, and you shall go and pray unto Me, and I will hearken unto you. And you shall seek Me, and find Me, when you shall search for Me, with all of your heart. And I will be found of you, saith the Lord; and I will turn away your captivity --- "

God is talking to Israel at a time when they were in serious trouble. They had been unfaithful and rebellious to God and the end result was, they ended up in captivity and under persecution of their enemy.

Why Would These Old Testament Scriptures Apply To Us/You/Me Today?

Because, God's principles of Promise and provision to His people, have been consistent, beginning with Adam and Eve until the Rapture occurs, and on into eternity.

God said in Hosea 4:6, "My people are destroyed for lack of knowledge—". Our lack of knowledge, in regard to God's grace, mercy, promise and provision have gotten us into similar circumstances like God's people were, hundreds of years ago. We haven't learned and practiced His principle of tithing, and giving, and simply learning to live within our means, not trying to keep up with the Jones'. Not learning to be content with what we have.

So our captivity today would be, not understanding and practicing, God's principles of money and time management and not tithing. Most of us have buried ourselves in debt. It is a FACT, that, Ninety percent (90%) of marriage and family related problems are on financial related issues.

SO, WHAT ABOUT TITHING?
Page 2

Let Us Review Some Old Testament Scriptures On Tithing.

God began the principle of tithing with Adam and Eve. Cain and Abel, their two sons, had the same responsibility to tithe as their parents did.

When it came time for them to tithe, Cain chose to give to God his way, rather than following God's specific instructions. God did not accept Cain's offering and Cain became very angry and jealous of his brother, because God had accepted Abel's offering. Cain killed his brother because of his own lack of understanding in regard to God's instructions and his own selfish ways.

Continuing in the Old Testament, we see that Abraham paid (a tenth part) tithes to Melchizedek, also known as, the King of Righteousness, and after that the King of Salem, which is the King of Peace. Genesis 14:20 and Hebrews 7:2.

Jacob made a pledge and said, "And this stone, which I have set for a pillar, shall be God's house: and all of that thou shalt give me, I will surely give the tenth unto thee". Genesis 28:22

Israel was instructed to tithe, and they were told that the tithe belongs to the Lord. They were also instructed, as to where to bring the tithe. The tithe was God's provision for His priest and other workers, to full fill the needs of His Temple. The Priest did not receive a portion of land for them selves when God was delegating land in the Promised land. Their part was handled through the tithe. In Leviticus, God designated the tithe to supply His house and the needs of His workers in the house. God refereed to the tithe as being the workers inheritance.

The Tithing Principles Did Not End With The Law.

Under the New Covenant, the provision for God's house is still the same. The Lord said, "A worker is worthy of his hire". The tithes paid to the Church, were designed by God to pay His servants for their work. This is how God covers the needs of His preachers, pastors, evangelist, secretaries, and all of the others that are in service to the Lord.

SO, What About Tithing?
Page 3

There is a special promise and blessing to those who tithe.

"Bring ye all the tithes into the store house, that there may be meat in mine house, and PROVE Me now herewith, saith the Lord of Hosts, if I will not open you the windows of heaven, and pour you out a blessing, that there shall not be room enough to receive it".
Malachi 3:10

The book of Deuteronomy in the Old Testament is referred to as the Blessing and Cursing warnings from God. He is saying if you follow my instructions, you will have my provisions and blessings in every area of your life. If you refuse My instructions and guidance, then curses will come upon you and you have chose to take yourself out from under My protection and provision. You will pay a price for making your own uninformed decisions.

How do we receive God's blessings and have balance in our life?

We must learn to live within our means, putting our priorities in order, as to our needs, and our wants, etc. We are instructed to be good stewards of our time and money so that we may be able to tithe. All things that pertain to us, increase and balance out in relation to our growth in the Word and spiritual maturity.
(APPLICATION OF THE WORD)

God loves a cheerful giver. Our attitude of contentment and trusting the Lord, is the source of TRUE PEACE AND JOY, learning to be content with what we have.

- We should first ask the Lord to forgive us, of our lack of understanding concerning tithing. I John 1:9
- The book of James says, "If any person lack wisdom, let him pray to the Father and He will give him wisdom liberally". James 1:2-6
- The book of James also says, that we don't know how to pray, because we want to satisfy our lust with our prayer request. James 4:3
- We should take a NEW LOOK at, who we are, and what we want and what our priorities are, and then ask the Lord to help us put our priorities in the correct order.

SO, What About Tithing?
Page 4

- Find a good money management program and put it into operation.
- Destroy virtually all your credit cards and pay off the balances as quickly as possible.
- Continue to ask God for the wisdom to manage your finances.
- Ask God to help you to begin tithing.
- The "First Fruits" imply, tithing off of the gross income, which is a simple 10%.
- Prepare you budget on of the remaining 90% of your income.
- In the New Testament, Jesus spoke of the tithe and said, "we should tithe". Giving to the Lord is part of, laying up for ourselves, treasure in heaven. Matthew 6:19-20
- Paul talked about, gathering the tithe on the first day of the week.

Learning God's principle of giving, helps us to understand, that we are a part of His plan, and a co-laborer with Him. Then we can become the cheerful giver Paul talks about in I Corinthians 9:7.

In Philippians 4:19 we are instructed, **"GOD WILL SUPPLY ALL OF OUR NEEDS, ACCORDING TO HIS RICHES IN GLORY"**.

In II Peter 3:18, we are told to **"GROW IN GRACE AND IN THE KNOWLEDGE OF OUR LORD AND SAVIOR JESUS CHRIST"**.

LEARN TO TRUST THE LORD FOR YOUR NEEDS.

FAITH HELPS

MEMORY WORK

Romans 3:23 — For all have sinned and come short of the glory of God.

John 3:16 — For God so loved the world that He gave His only begotten Son, that whosoever believeth in Him should not perish but have everlasting life.

Romans 10:9-10 — That if thou shalt confess with thy mouth the Lord Jesus and shalt believe in thy heart that God has raised Him from the dead, thou shalt be saved. For with the heart man believeth unto righteousness, and with the mouth confession is made unto salvation. (THIS IS THE FOUNDATION, FOR EVERYTHING THAT WE   RECEIVE FROM GOD).

Ephesians 2:8-9 — For by grace are you saved through faith and that not of yourselves, it is the gift of God, Not of works, lest any man should boast. Look at page 73, WORK OUT YOUR OWN SALVATION.

Romans 10:17 — So then faith cometh by hearing, and hearing by the Word (Rhema) of God.

II Timothy 2:15 — Study to show thyself approved unto God, a workman that needeth not to be ashamed, rightly dividing the word of truth. Look at page 19, point number 11. Use, 3-7 sets of scripture, to confirm a point in the Word.

Psalm 119:11 — Thy Word have I hid in my heart that I might not sin against thee.

Galatians 5:22-23- But the FRUIT OF THE SPIRIT is LOVE, JOY, PEACE, LONGSUFFERING, GENTLENESS, GOODNESS, FAITH, MEEKNESS, TEMPERANCE; against such there is no law.

James 1:21-22 — Be ye doers of the Word and not hearers only.

Psalm 19:14 — Let the words of my mouth and the meditation of my heart be acceptable in thy sight, O Lord, my strength and my redeemer.

John 15:7 — If ye abide in me, and my words (Rhema) abide in you, ye shall ask what ye will, and it shall be done unto you. Look at page 20, HOW TO SIFT GOD'S WORD FROM THE HEAD TO THE HEART.

John 16:24 — Hitherto have ye asked nothing in my name: ask and ye shall receive that your joy may be full.

Matthew 6:33 — But seek ye first the kingdom of God and His righteousness, and all these things will be added unto you.

Hebrews 11:6 — But without faith it is impossible to please Him, for God is a **re-warder** of them that **diligently seek Him**.

"COME UNTO ME"
WORDS TO REMEMBER

God's *THOUGHTS* toward us. LOOK UP AND READ, Jeremiah 29:11-14.

Behold, I stand at the door and knock. If any man *HEARS* my voice and *OPENS* the door, I will come in to him and will sup with him, and he with Me. (RELATIONSHIP AND FELLOWSHIP) Revelation 3:20

SEEK ye *FIRST* the kingdom of God and *His* righteousness and *ALL* these things *SHALL* be added unto you. Matthew 6:33

COME unto me, and I will *GIVE you REST*. Matthew 11:28

MEDITATE on God's *Word* day and night--*AND YOU WILL BE A GOOD SUCCESS.* **Joshua 1:8**

God is **LOOKING** for people to **WORSHIP HIM IN SPIRIT AND TRUTH**. John 4:21-24

But they that *WAIT UPON* the Lord *SHALL RENEW THEIR STRENGTH ---*. Isaiah 40:31

WAIT FOR THE PROMISE OF THE FATHER --- Acts 1:4 - 8, Luke 3:16 and Luke 24:49

RIVERS of LIVING WATER shall flow OUT of you --. John 7:37-39

HOW MUCH MORE SHALL THE HEAVENLY FATHER GIVE THE HOLY SPIRIT TO THEM THAT ASK. Luke 11:13

So that the BLESSINGS of Abraham will come on the Gentiles also. Galatians 3:13-14

Perfect love casts out *ALL FEAR*. I John 4:18

For God *HATH* not given us the spirit of fear but *OF POWER AND LOVE AND OF A SOUND MIND.* II Timothy 1:7

THE KINGDOM OF GOD IS NOT MEAT AND DRINK BUT RIGHTEOUSNESS AND PEACE AND JOY IN THE HOLY SPIRIT,

Romans 14:17. Look at, WHAT IS, GOD'S SNUGGLE PACKAGE?

FAITH BUILDERS #1

1. GOD HEARS OUR PRAYER (I Peter 3:12).

2. This is the confidence that we have in our Father, that if we ask anything according to His will, He hears us. And we know that He hears us, and whatsoever we ask, we know that we have the petitions that we desired of Him (I John 5:14-15). Review, How To Approach God, in the Prayer Study.

3. If you abide in Me and My Words (Rhema) abide in you, you shall ask what you will, and it shall be done unto you (John 15:7).

4. A FAITH STATEMENT: When I walk in the Word (Rhema), my Father backs up His Word. Whatever I ask in Jesus' name will come to pass.

5.   FACT ------------FAITH ------------ FEELINGS
      (THE WORD)   (TRUST)   (WHEN THE ANSWER COMES)

              DO NOT WALK BY FEELINGS

6. REMEMBER, WE ARE UNDER THE NEW COVENANT. GOD SAY'S **YES**, TO **TOTAL** REDEMPTION, **SPIRIT, SOUL, and BODY**.

7. BE IT UNTO YOU ACCORDING TO YOUR FAITH (Matthew 9:29).

8. WITH GOD, NOTHING SHALL BE IMPOSSIBLE (Luke 1:37).

9. IS THERE ANYTHING TOO HARD FOR ME (Jeremiah 32:27)?

10. A FAITH STATEMENT: HEALING POWER IS ALWAYS PRESENT--LOOK AT THE SITUATION THROUGH EYES OF FAITH. GREATER IS HE THAT IS IN YOU; I John 4:4 and LOOK UNTO JESUS, the AUTHOR and FINISHER of your FAITH, Hebrews 12:2

11. HAVE FAITH IN GOD: For verily I say unto you, That whosoever shall say unto this mountain, be thou removed, and be thou cast into the sea; and shall not doubt in his heart, but shall believe that those things which he saith shall come to pass; he shall have whatsoever he saith. Therefore, I say unto YOU, What things soever YOU DESIRE, when YOU PRAY, BELIEVE THAT YOU RECEIVE THEM, AND YOU SHALL HAVE THEM (Mark 11:23-24 and Romans 10:9-10 and pages 56-58).

THE PERSON WHO SAVES YOU AND HEALS YOU, LIVES IN YOU.

12. YOU MUST FORGIVE, Mark 11:25-26. CAST ALL OF YOUR CARE UPON HIM BECAUSE HE CARES FOR YOU, I Peter 5:7.

FAITH BUILDERS #2

NOTE: THESE STUDIES ARE TO LIFT OUR FAITH.
THEY ARE NOT A SUBSTITUTE FOR OUR FAITH.

WHAT ARE OUR GOALS?

1. Learn To Compare Ourselves To Jesus And Not To Others

    a. Read Acts 10:38 and remember Jesus said, "As the Father sent Me."
    b. Read Hebrews 2:17 and II Corinthians 5:18. We are ministers of reconciliation.

2. Compare ourselves to the Book of Acts to see if we really have heard what Jesus said. Acts 1:8 and 5:42; Galatians 5:1-26; Mark 16:14-20--also the Gospels where Jesus sent out the twelve TWO-BY-TWO and then the seventy others out, TWO-BY-TWO.

3. Examine ourselves to see what adjustments need to be made for us to become conscious of the indwelling Holy Spirit, and let Him guide--lead and teach us (Romans 8:8-17; Romans 12:1-2; Galatians 5:13-26; John 3:3; John 7:37-39).

4. Learn Who We Are In The Kingdom Of God

    a. Romans 8:17 - We are a joint HEIR.
    b. We do not belong to this world (John 17:16; Romans 14:17-19).
    c. Everything that Jesus has He has given to His BRIDE, THE CHURCH.

5. Seek And Find All The Fringe Benefits As A JOINT HEIR To Jesus

    a. Philippians 4:19 - All things!
    b. Galatians 3:13-14 - More promises.
    c. I Corinthians 12:31 - Covet earnestly the best gifts.
    d. Hebrews 4:16 - COME BOLDLY TO THE THRONE OF GRACE.

6. Learn How To Recognize And Deal With Our Enemy God's Way

    a. I Peter 5:8 - Notice the enemy roars like a lion; He is not THE LION.
    b. Ephesians 6:10-18 - Gospel armor.
    c. II Corinthians 10:3-6 - Weapons of warfare.
    d. Romans 8:37 - More than conquerors.

7. Learn To Walk With Peace And Joy Even Under Pressure

    a. John 14:27 - Jesus said, "Peace I give unto you."
    b. James 1:12 - Endureth temptation.

STRESS OR PEACE OF MIND

Isaiah 40:31	Wait upon the Lord.
John 14:27	My peace I give to you.
Isaiah 26:3	Keep your mind on Him.
Philippians 4:1-23	Think on these things.
Romans 14:17	The kingdom of God is peace and joy in the Holy Spirit.
II Timothy 1:7	God did not give us a spirit of fear, but of power, love, and a sound mind. Review IN HIM
Galatians 5:18:26	God's character—the fruit of the spirit.
Jeremiah 33:3	The Lord's phone number.
I Peter 5:6-11	Cast all your care upon Him because He cares for you.
II Peter 2:9	Our Father does not want you to remain in abusive or dangerous situations. The Lord knows how to deliver you out of a harmful situation.
II Corinthians 10:3-7,	The weapons of our warfare are spiritual for victory over the enemy. Look at THE NEW COVENANT AUTHORITY. You may also review "COME UNTO ME"

GOD GIVES THE BEST TO THOSE

WHO LEAVE THE CHOICE TO HIM.

YOUR HEAVENLY FATHER WANTS YOU TO REMEMBER

We have been invited by the Father to be INVOLVED IN His life, and He WANTS TO BE INVOLVED IN OUR LIFE.

BY BEING BORN AGAIN WE HAVE DIRECT ACCESS TO OUR FATHER AND OUR LORD AND SAVIOR JESUS CHRIST.

The SEED of the Father's character and nature were planted in our spirit by the Holy Spirit when we were, Born-Again, II Peter 1:2-11

The HARVEST of YOUR FRUIT depends on how much you ALLOW THE HOLY SPIRIT TO WATER your spirit (John 7:37-39).

WE KNOW GOD TO THE DEGREE THAT WE KNOW HIS WORD.

SNUGGLE - SNUGGLE - SNUGGLE

How much more shall the Father give the Holy Spirit to them that ask (Luke 11:13).

The way we live our life depends on how much we ALLOW THE HOLY SPIRIT TO APPLY THE LIVING WATER.

THIS IS THE PRIMARY PURPOSE OF, THE PROMISE OF THE FATHER.

REMEMBER: GOD LOVES YOU!

JUDE

From: Jude, a servant of Jesus Christ, and a brother of James.

To: Christians everywhere, for God the Father has chosen you and Jesus Christ has kept you safe.

2. May you be given more and more of God's kindness, peace, and love.

3. Dearly loved friends, I had been planning to write you some thoughts about the salvation God has given us, but now I find I must write of something else instead, urging you to stoutly defend the truth which God gave, once for all, to His people to keep without change through the years.

4. I say this because some godless teachers have wormed their way in among you, saying that after we become Christians we can do just as we like without fear of God's punishment. The fate of such people was written long ago, for they have turned against our only master and Lord, Jesus Christ.

5. My answer to them is: remember this fact-which you know already-that the Lord saved a whole nation of people out of the land of Egypt, and then killed every one of them who did not trust and obey Him.

6. And I remind you of those angels who were once pure and holy, but willingly turned to a life of sin. Now God has them chained up in prisons of darkness, waiting for the judgment day.

7. And don't forget the cities of Sodom and Gomorrah and their neighboring towns, all full of lust of every kind including lust of men for other men. Those cities were destroyed by fire and continue to be a warning to us that there is a hell in which sinners are punished.

8. Yet these false teachers go on living their evil, immoral lives, degrading their bodies and laughing at those in authority over them, even scoffing at the Glorious Ones (those mighty powers of awful evil who left their first estate).

9. Yet Michael, one of the mightiest of the angles, when he was arguing with Satan about Moses' body, did not dare to accuse Satan, or jeer at him, but simply said, "The Lord

10. But these men mock and curse at anything they do not understand, and, like animals, they do whatever they feel like, thereby ruining their souls.

11. Woe upon them! For they follow the example of Cain who killed his brother; and, like Balaam, they will do anything for money; and like Korah, they have disobeyed God in the hope of gain and will die under His curse.

12. When these men join you at the love feasts of the church, they are evil smears among you, laughing and carrying on, gorging and stuffing themselves without a thought for others. They are like clouds blowing over dry land without giving rain, promising much, but producing nothing. They are like fruit trees without any fruit at picking time. They are not only dead, but doubly dead, for they have been pulled out, roots and all, to be burned.

JUDE - Cont.

13. All they leave behind them is shame and disgrace like the dirty foam along the beach left by the wild waves. They wander around looking as bright as stars, but ahead of them is the everlasting gloom and darkness that God has prepared for them.

14. Enoch, who lived long ago, soon after Adam, knew about these men and said this about them: "See, the Lord is coming with millions of His holy ones".

15. He will bring the people of the world before Him in judgment, to receive just punishment, and to prove the terrible things they have done in rebellion against God, revealing all they have said against Him."

16. These men are constant grippers, never satisfied, doing whatever evil they feel like; they are loud-mouthed "show-off's," and when they show respect for others, it is only to get something from them in return.

17. Dear friends, remember what the apostles of our Lord Jesus Christ told you,

18. That in the last times there would come these scoffers whose whole purpose in life is to enjoy themselves in every evil way imaginable.

19. They stir up arguments; they love the evil things of the world; they do not have the Holy Spirit living in them.

20. But you, dear friends, must build up your lives ever more strongly upon the foundations of our *HOLY FAITH, LEARNING TO PRAY IN THE POWER AND STRENGTH OF THE HOLY SPIRIT.*

21. Stay always within the boundaries where God's love can reach and bless you. Wait patiently for the eternal life that our Lord Jesus Christ in His mercy is going to give you.

22. Try to help those who argue against you. Be merciful to those who doubt.

23. Save some by snatching them as from the very flames of hell itself. And as for others, help them to find the Lord by being kind to them, but be careful that you yourselves aren't pulled along into their sins. Hate every trace of their sin while being merciful to them as sinners.

24-25. And now-- all glory to Him who alone is God, who saves us through Jesus Christ our Lord; Yes splendor and majesty, all power and authority are His from the beginning; His they are and His they evermore shall be. And He is
    able to keep you from slipping and falling away, and to bring you, sinless and perfect into His glorious presence with mighty shouts everlasting joy. AMEN. Jude

Scripture quotations are taken from *The Living Bible*, copyright 1971. Used by permission of Tyndale House Publishers Inc. Wheaton IL 60989.
All rights reserved.

THE TEN COMMANDMENTS
EXODUS CHAPTER 20

1. THOU SHALT HAVE NO OTHER GODS BEFORE ME.

2. THOU SHALT NOT MAKE UNTO THEE ANY GRAVEN IMAGE.

3. THOU SHALT NOT TAKE THE NAME OF THE LORD IN VANE.

4. REMEMBER THE SABBATH DAY, TO KEEP IT HOLY.

5. HONOR THY FATHER AND THY MOTHER.

6. THOU SHALT NOT KILL.

7. THOU SHALT NOT COMMIT ADULTERY.

8. THOU SHALT NOT STEAL.

9. THOU SHALT NOT BEAR FALSE WITNESS.

10. THOU SHALT NOT COVET.

Note;

When you are Born-Again and you are being led by the Holy Spirit, you are living on a higher level of life compared to, the people that lived under LAW.

Paul is teaching the amazing difference, between the Law and Grace, in the book of Galatians.

You Can Receive Eternal Life...Right Now

God's Gift package begins the moment you become a child of God.
The package has benefits that cover us while we are here on earth, such as, **ETERNAL LIFE, ETERNAL RETIREMENT AND FORGIVENESS OF ALL OUR SINS.**

Then a major package begins when we go to heaven.

This brochure shares how to begin as a child of God by coming to Him on His terms through His Son Jesus.

QUESTION ?
Do you believe that Jesus is the Son of God?

THE KEY VERSE IN THE BIBLE:
"But these are written, that you might believe that Jesus is the Christ, the Son of God; and that believing you might have life through His Name." John 20:31 (KJV)

QUESTION ?
Do you know how much God loves YOU ?

"For God so loved the World, that He gave His only begotten Son, that whosoever believeth in Him should not perish, but have everlasting life." John 3:16 (KJV)

Now, let's personalize this verse by placing your name in the blanks:

For God so loved_____, that He gave His only begotten Son, that (if) _____ believeth in Him, (then)_____ should not perish, but _____ (will) have everlasting life.

QUESTION ?
Do you know that the cancer of the soul, called sin, has touched every human being, causing complete separation from God ?
"For all have sinned, and fall short of the Glory of God."
Romans 3:23 (KJV)

QUESTION ?
Do you realize that sin causes you spirit to die ? But, do you realize that God's GIFT of salvation will cause your spirit to live forever ?

HAVE YOU MADE YOUR CHOICE ?

"For the wages of sin is death; **but the Gift of God is eternal life through Jesus Christ our Lord.**" Romans 6:23 (KJV)

QUESTION ?
Do you know how much God desires your friendship ?

"Behold, I stand at the door and knock; if anyone hears my voice, and opens the door, I will come into him, and will sup with him, and he with me." Revelation 3:20   (KJV)

QUESTION ?
What is your next step ? Simply ask Him to be your Savior !
It's simple. Just ask Him !

"For whosoever shall call upon the name of the Lord, shall be saved." Romans 10:13 (KJV)

Dear Jesus, forgive me all my sins and save my soul. I repent of my sins and ask you to come into my heart and be the Lord of my life. Take control of my life, for I give myself to You now. Thank You for hearing my prayer and for saving soul. In Jesus Name, I pray.

YOU ARE SAVED BY GRACE THROUGH FAITH

"For by Grace you have been saved through Faith, and not of yourselves; it is the Gift of God, not of works, lest anyone should boast." Ephesians 2:8-9 (KJV)

ETERNAL LIFE IS PROMISED

"Most assuredly, I say to you, he who hears My Word and believes in Him who sent Me has everlasting life, and shall not come into judgment, but has passed from death into life." John 5:24 (KJV)

"And this is the testimony; that God has given us eternal life, and this life is in His Son. He who has the Son has life; he who does not have the Son of God does not have life." I John 5:11-12 (KJV)

"These things I have written to you who believe in the name of the Son of God, that you MAY KNOW that you HAVE ETERNAL LIFE."
I John 5:13 (KJV)

NOTES

www.ingramcontent.com/pod-product-compliance
Lightning Source LLC
Chambersburg PA
CBHW031957080426
42735CB00007B/430